D0389403

If 7:14

If my people, which are calle
by my name, shall humble themselve
and pray
and seek my face, and turn from the
wicked ways; then will I hear fro
heaven, and will forgive their si
and will heal their land

If 7:14

An Urgent Call for Revival...It's Time

Bob Vander Plaats

If 7:14

Literary development and design: Koechel Peterson & Associates, Inc., Minneapolis, Minnesota.

Books may be ordered by contacting:

The FAMiLY LEADER
P.O. Box 42245
Urbandale, IA 50323
515.263.3495
TheFamilyLeader.com

ISBN 978-0-9910264-0-1

Printed in the United States of America

If 7:14

dedication

To
all those
who vow to say
"I will…"

acknowledgments

We acknowledge . . .

THE GOD OF THE UNIVERSE, who is our Hope and who provides the "2 Chronicles 7:14" template for revival in His Holy Word.

The FAMiLY LEADER Board for their vision and leadership . . . always persevering to impact our culture with truth . . . in love. Specifically, we acknowledge Director Dave Kutscher and his wife, Cheryl, for prompting, confirming, propelling, and knitting together the "If 7:14" vision.

The FAMiLY LEADER Team . . . I am biased, but I truly believe The FAMiLY LEADER's team is the best! Their engaged interest and wise insight and contribution were invaluable as we dissected 2 Chronicles 7:14 together. I truly believe *If 7:14* is blessed through their prayers, their voice, their enhanced edits, and their constant encouragement.

JOEL ROSENBERG . . . a newfound friend whose passionate conversations in a hotel lobby, during car rides, and at the 2012 FAMiLY LEADERSHIP Summit helped birth The FAMiLY LEADER's "If 7:14" vision.

Mike Huckabee . . . for not truncating his timely "revival" message at our 2012 FAMiLY LEADERSHIP Summit, and for providing the bold and clear Foreword for *If 7:14*.

Mike and Cheryl Wells for their passionate and persevering hearts for revival.

The Publishing Team represented by Koechel Peterson and Associates.

> John Peterson for his publishing leadership.
> David Koechel for *If 7:14*'s art direction and design.
> Lance Wubbels for his editing.

Pastors Mike Householder and Jeff Moes. They were the first to read the "draft" manuscript. Their friendship, their encouragement, and their theological insight are a great blessing.

And, to my wife, Darla, for being with me for thirty years and who, along with our four boys, loves me, encourages me, inspires me, and challenges me.

contents

WHILE *I COULD* WAX ELOQUENT and sentimental about my friendship with the author, Bob Vander Plaats, the happy memories of winning the Iowa Caucuses with his help, and the numerous, enthusiastic FAMiLY LEADER events he's invited me to headline, *I won't*—simply because the hour is too late, and the topic is too urgent.

You see, this book is one I'd happily recommend even if my worst enemy had written it! That's because it forcefully reminds us that without spiritual revival, this country is "game over"; and it perfectly delivers the ways and means to that necessary revival.

As I said at last year's Family Leadership Summit, our nation's problems, and their solutions, are ultimately *spiritual* rather than political.

That doesn't mean Bob's, and my, and many others' efforts to restore this "great American experiment in ordered liberty" are pointless. It just means that, unless those efforts are preceded by, and rooted in, our relationship with the Lawgiver; and unless those efforts are done His way, for His glory; then those efforts will ultimately "succeed no better than the builders of Babel," as Benjamin Franklin so poignantly observed.

We've *got* to get this right! Contrary to the modern secular myth, *of course* Church and State are connected! God created them both and expects both to function properly and complement each other.

Of course successful civil government needs biblical faith to suffuse it. George Washington said, "It is impossible to rightly govern without God and the Bible." He also essentially said in his "Magnum Opus" (Farewell Address) that we would commit national suicide if we tried to separate the two.

Well, Bob has identified that suicidal separation occurring today, diagnosed its root causes, and prescribed the only remedies God will countenance: humbly praying, intimately seeking God, and authentically turning away from our sins.

So yes, we *can* do civics and Christianity simultaneously—we can *walk* and chew gum at the same time. But we need to be *awake* to do them both well. Hence, Bob makes this clarion call for the *Church to come awake*—humbly, prayerfully, and repentantly. Then and only then will we get our civics back on track.

With that clear, profound call before us, I'll end this Foreword with an old saying I heard many years ago from a wise Christian: "The Church of Jesus Christ will only move *forward on its knees." Won't you make the decision* to join Bob, me, and perhaps millions of others, in accepting God's offer to forgive our sins and heal our land, *"If" we will do our part,* on our knees?

Governor Mike Huckabee

"If my people,
who are called
by my name, will humble
themselves and pray
and seek my face and
turn from their
wicked ways, then I will
hear from heaven,
and I will forgive their sin
and will heal their land."

2 CHRONICLES 7:14

As I write this, our government is "shut down." It is shut down because there is a lack of faith in our government, in our process, and an erosion of trust in our leaders and politicians. All signs point to, "There's got to be something more!" The good news is . . . there is something more!

Our faith isn't in government nor is our trust in an earthly king. Our faith is in the One who instituted government, who rules over all, who is King of kings and Lord of lords. He is the Alpha and the Omega . . . the beginning and the end.

Welcome to *If 7:14*!

On August 11, 2012, The FAMiLY LEADER's first annual "Family Leadership Summit" welcomed spiritual leaders such as Joel Rosenberg and Dr. Laurence White. We wanted our team of supporters to be girded with a biblical worldview as we addressed the issues that impact our culture. Emphasizing the worldview application were Iowa's two back-to-back presidential caucus winners, Mike Huckabee and Rick Santorum, along with Texas governor, Rick Perry.

We had an outstanding lineup, and the venue was "sold out." People from various states showed up early and left late. They were hungry to do something . . . anything . . . to make a difference in a culture that they saw spinning out of control. After approximately seven hours, several speakers, and a surprise "Huckabee Show" live from our event, attendees left inspired, stirred, and wanting more.

The message was clear. Our only hope in turning things around spiritually, fiscally, morally, locally, internationally, and personally is . . . revival. Speaker after speaker stepped up to the podium and delivered this call for revival as our ultimate hope, each in his own words, with his own stories, his own experiences, and his own leadership outlooks.

Frankly, I wasn't prepared for this unplanned but well-orchestrated message. We had elections on the horizon. And as it seems with every election, this was "the most important election of our lifetimes." The White House, the Senate, governorships, and statehouses were all up for grabs, and we all felt the pressure of the assumption that we needed to win "if" there was to be any hope for the future . . . for our country, for our states, for our communities, for our families, for us.

While each speaker recognized the importance of elections, they all pointed to and passionately emphasized something more . . . revival.

Texas governor, Rick Perry, said, "We [meaning Christians, God's people, who bear His name] must do more than bring change to Washington, D.C. . . . We must lead the next 'Great Awakening' for America." He said that policies and politicians will change, blowing in the proverbial polling winds. However, true and lasting change is only realized through an authentic and vibrant "Spiritual Awakening." Wow!

A white-collared Lutheran pastor named Laurence White from Texas followed his governor and admonished believers, stating, "Instead of transforming the world, the world has transformed the Church. We live by the same twisted, perverted standards as advocated by the ungodly all around us." You could have heard a pin drop. This blunt and forceful preacher didn't for a second suggest that our cure would be found in politics. It would only be realized when "the Church would truly be the Church . . . by letting our 'light' shine . . . through fresh salt . . . and through the only strategy that truly sets men free—the truth!"

The attendees sat silent . . . then rose in unison with a vigorous standing ovation. His words peeled back the onion and uncovered the masks of comfortable convenience as he challenged the Church to rise up and be the Church!

As we attempted to catch our collective breaths, author Joel Rosenberg came to the microphone. His message, entitled "Can America Survive the Current Fiscal and Spiritual Crisis?" was one that we all were looking forward to. I, for one, was looking for the ideal leader and the necessary strategies to right our national ship.

Rosenberg's answer was not founded in a personality nor was it grounded in specific, strategic policies. Rather, it was rooted in revival.

He shifted our focus with a most uncomfortable question, "Is America in trouble because of the pagans, or is

America in trouble because of the Church?" The only sound in response to that question was nervous shifting of people in the auditorium seats.

Not letting up, his next question was equally pointed, "Where are you?" He made it personal. The answer to our fiscal and spiritual survival as a country must flow through me . . . through you . . . through us.

His concluding remarks emphasized the sincerity of his message, as he spurred the audience toward personal accountability and revival with, "If we beg God as individuals, as families, as congregations . . . plead with Him, fast, pray . . . plead with God the Father to apply 2 Chronicles 7:14 to our country, the United States, He might do it."

After Rosenberg's message, we realized that if we had showed up hoping to pin our nation's shortcomings on our political opposition and to blame others for our collapsing spin, we had come to the wrong place. Message after message was calling us to account. We need revival.

While the day was exceptionally inspirational, I was confident that our final two speakers would deliver the "political hope" that many had come to hear. The last two Iowa caucus winners were up next.

Senator Rick Santorum and Governor Mike Huckabee didn't have the privilege of listening to the previous speakers. Providentially, they repeated the God-ordained message. We need revival.

With great precision, Senator Santorum detailed the uphill climb and unprecedented challenges we face as a country. His solution was to point out our need for an unprecedented revival that "returns us to the values that made this country great."

Former Baptist pastor, Arkansas Governor, presidential candidate, and television/radio personality Mike Huckabee was the final speaker, and by now the message was personally sinking in. I prepared myself to listen to Pastor Huckabee instead of Governor Huckabee.

The former pastor was clearly at home with this audience, and his mission and message were clear: we must collectively turn our hearts back to God. He dialed in the focus of his speech immediately when he stated, "Until we as a country get back to our place where we understand that we are a nation under God, conceived by His own grace and purpose, and, when we turn our backs on His purpose and His providence, it doesn't matter whom we elect, we will still be wanting and wishing and we will not be the great nation that we were designed and destined to be. Ultimately, this is not a political problem . . . it is a spiritual problem."

The crowd cheered at his remarks. It was as if they were turning their minds and hearts away from the negative television ads while embracing God's call for revival. Sensing this embrace, Huckabee referenced 1 Kings 19 and challenged us to come out from under the juniper tree as did Elijah after all hope was gone.

He reminded us, "We are not alone. If you listen to that still small voice of God, you will realize He has many people who've not bowed their knee to Baal." Then with all the urgency he could muster, he again reminded us, "You are not alone!"

And in case we still didn't get it, once again via his closing remarks, he said, "But even if you were all alone, it'd be a whole lot better for you to have God on your side versus you being with all the others and God being on the other side. You are not alone!"

This focus on revival should not have been new to me or to the audience. However, it was. It was fresh. It was relevant. It was inspiring. It was authentic.

It's God's heart!

Following the Summit, our board, our team, and I reflected intentionally and prayerfully on this need for revival. Birthed from this reflection is this book, *If 7:14,* and, as you will read in the "Call to Action," our "If 7:14 Initiative."

As you read the following chapters that unpack 2 Chronicles 7:14, please know that I need revival. My heart needs revival. My mind needs revival. My marriage needs revival. My family needs revival. My church needs revival. I write these words not just to you, but to me. It is my hope that as I intentionally renew, as Darla and I recommit, as our family refocuses, and as our church reawakens . . . you will find encouragement and inspiration.

We are not alone. But revival begins with you . . . with me . . . with us.

Let's begin . . . *If 7:14* . . . it's time!

CHAPTER ONE

"IF"

If God is for us,
who is against us?

ROMANS 8:31 NASB

CHAPTER ONE

"If"

My fourth grade teacher, who was all of 4'11", was fond of saying, "Dynamite comes in small packages." Nothing could be more descriptive of this concept than the little two-letter word *if.*

I never gave much thought to this word until our team at The FAMiLY LEADER decided to dissect each word and phrase of 2 Chronicles 7:14. We believe this verse, although not strictly directed at the United States of America, provides a glimpse into God's heart and, thus, a template for a nation's revival.

I've heard and used the word *if* on many occasions and in a variety of circumstances. It may just be the most challenging word in the English language. Its very utterance prompts one to make a decision. The receiver of the word has a choice to make. The voice of the word is looking for action.

In the New International Version of the Holy Bible, the word *if* is used over fifteen hundred times. The word *if* either follows a promise or is a predicate to a promise.

However, the promise or the result or the consequence is predicated on a choice.

To illustrate this point and the power of *if*, let's pick up the infamous story of Sodom and Gomorrah in Genesis 18, beginning at verse 22 and ending at verse 33:

The men turned away and went toward Sodom, but Abraham remained standing before the LORD. Then Abraham approached him and said: "Will you sweep away the righteous with the wicked? What if there are fifty righteous people in the city? Will you really sweep it away and not spare the place for the sake of the fifty righteous people in it? Far be it from you to do such a thing—to kill the righteous with the wicked, treating the righteous and the wicked alike. Far be it from you! Will not the Judge of all the earth do right?"

The LORD said, "If I find fifty righteous people in the city of Sodom, I will spare the whole place for their sake."

Then Abraham spoke up again: "Now that I have been so bold as to speak to the Lord, though I am nothing but dust and ashes, what if the number of the righteous is five less than fifty? Will you destroy the whole city for lack of five people?"

"If I find forty-five there," he said, "I will not destroy it."

Once again he spoke to him, "What if only forty are found there?"

He said, "For the sake of forty, I will not do it."

Then he said, "May the Lord not be angry, but let me speak. What if only thirty can be found there?"

He answered, "I will not do it if I find thirty there."

Abraham said, "Now that I have been so bold as to speak to the Lord, what if only twenty can be found there?"

He said, "For the sake of twenty, I will not destroy it."

Then he said, "May the Lord not be angry, but let me speak just once more. What if only ten can be found there?"

He answered, "For the sake of ten, I will not destroy it."

When the LORD had finished speaking with Abraham, he left, and Abraham returned home.

Wow, this little word *if* turned into a major bargaining chip. Abraham negotiates the number of righteous in the sinful city from 50 to 45 to 40 to 30 to 20 to 10. Abraham includes repeated *ifs* in his questions to God, and God recites the repeated *ifs* in His answers. The net sum is, "Just find Me a small and committed core of righteous people, and I will spare the land."

That message in and of itself should be encouragement enough for America. In high stakes negotiations, we are offered great insight regarding the character of God. He doesn't need the whole city to be found righteous, not even a majority. He is just asking for a small core to work with and to build from who earnestly are seeking and living out righteousness. Maybe we need to take a lesson from Abraham and pray that God will find a small core of righteous men and women to spare our nation from rightful judgment and commence a modern-day revival.

Now, back to the word *if.* I've been a teacher, a coach, a parent, and a leader in business, politics, and ministry. As I contemplate this two-letter gem, I am fascinated by its usage. Follow along with these examples as you consider the importance of the intentional beginning of this revival verse.

As a parent, I'm sure you recognize the power of *if.* "If you eat all your vegetables, I will give you two scoops of ice cream." I realize there is a great dichotomy in this challenge, but I know many parents who have reached for much greater and much more despicable vegetable eating techniques than two scoops of ice cream. We've all heard, "If you clean your plate, you can have dessert."

Why the *if*? It is a motivational technique used on children to get them to eat what is healthy and good for them. The hope of the *if* is that when children begin the habit of eating their greens and their carrots, they will grow a liking for them and, thus, make healthy eating decisions as they mature.

As a matter of fact, the power of *if* is a parenting staple. See if you have heard of this one. "If you take a bath and put on your pajamas without a fuss, I will read you a bedtime story." Or how about, "If you sit still throughout the whole church service, I will give you a dollar"? The *if* is the behavior we desire, and bedtime stories and cash are the motivators for proper behavior.

Parenting is about creating an environment and a desire to make right choices, and this little word is the prompter for results.

My friends have given me a bad time for not giving my boys a choice when it comes to playing basketball. They believe I have forced this game upon them. I am steadfast in my defense. I most certainly give them a choice. *If* they want to eat, they'll practice. *If* they don't want to eat, they don't have to practice. For those who know me, you're smiling now. The choice is theirs, and it's all precipitated with the word *if*.

Teachers, coaches, and leaders of all disciplines and strategy resort to the word *if* frequently to obtain desired results. Leaders of business tell their sales forces routinely that *if* they exceed their quotas, substantial bonuses await them at the end of each quarter and fiscal year.

Coaches tell their players that *if* they hit the weights, *if* they put in the shots, and *if* they adhere to scheduled conditioning, they will maximize their ability and the team's performance.

Teachers instruct their pupils to study, to read, and to prepare. And *if* the pupils put in the time and fundamentals of learning, they will succeed in any given curriculum offering.

If also represents a tipping point. *If* you do as the parent, as the teacher, as the coach, and as the leader recommends, you are going to experience fulfillment. However, *if* you choose to ignore or to defy, you will experience the consequences of obesity, of not making the grade or the team, or of being unemployed. The irony of the *if* is that it is up to you, to me, and to us to make the appropriate decision.

And *ifs* can have clear warnings that outline devastating consequences. Take Matthew 18:6 as an example: "*If* anyone causes one of these little ones—those who believe in me—to stumble, it would be better for them to have a large millstone hung around their neck and to be drowned in the depths of the sea." Wow, God's *if* demonstrates His love for and value of our children.

Our teaching and instruction are paramount in His eyes as we are given the mantle of parenting and nurturing. The *if* gets our attention, and what follows the *if* is a clarion warning of the high stakes of leadership and parenting.

And of all the *ifs* ever uttered, there is none more sincere and ultimately transformative than Christ's *if* in the garden of Gethsemane on the night before His crucifixion. Luke recounts these words in chapter 22:42: "Father, *if* you are willing, take this cup from me; yet not my will, but yours be done."

Jesus' *if* is directed toward God, His Father in heaven. Notice how He states His desire yet submits to the Father's ultimate will. How many times have we prayed for God to take our sickness, our financial circumstance, our disability, or our doubt from us? Jesus' prayer models permission to seek God for relief *if* our prayer is humbly and authentically predicated on our submission to God's will.

Of all the words God could have chosen to spur us on to revival, there is none greater than *if*. The *if* transitions the weight of responsibility. It encourages personal and corporate responsibility. It demands action, authenticity, and sincerity.

And God, just like the parent, the teacher, the coach, and the leader, is hoping we will make the right decision. As He states in Isaiah 48:18, "*If* only you had paid attention to my commands, your peace would have been like a river, your well-being like the waves of the sea."

My prayer is that we, as His people, pay attention.

"If only . . ."

CHAPTER 2

"MY PEOPLE"

I will give them a heart to know Me,
for I am the LORD;
and they will be My people,
and I will be their God,
for they will return to Me
with their whole heart.

JEREMIAH 24:7 NASB

"My People"

So, who are "My people"? We hear leaders make reference to "my people" frequently. Coaches say "my team." Parents say "my children." Pastors express "my congregation." And employers coin "my employees."

The "my" makes it possessive. "My" reflects headship and represents a flowchart of authority. The person behind the "my" is the leader who has the authority, the power, the final word or decision.

The word *people* represents a degree of subordination. The team is subordinate to the coach. The children are subordinate to the parents. The employees are subordinate to the boss. The cut-to-the-chase explanation is: Whatever the boss, the leader, the coach, or the parent says to do, to accomplish, or to maneuver, the team, the children, and the employees bear the responsibility and are held to account.

As I write this, our home in central Iowa is experiencing a blizzard of whopping proportions. Thirteen inches of snow and fifty mile per hour wind are a combination that makes even the toughest hunker down and huddle with their people, the ones they love . . . their family.

In addition, this storm is occurring less than a week prior to Christmas.

I'm fortunate. Darla and I have our four boys in close proximity, so we are enjoying a break from the hustle and bustle and enjoying our family. However, there are many trying to get home to their families. They are stranded on the interstates, in the ditches, or in unfamiliar hotels and surroundings.

Blizzards, along with other interruptions of nature, cause us to put in the proverbial clutch on the unimportant and focus on the important. The important for us is the safety of our homes, and for the stranded, is family.

When Darla and I are introduced to others, one of the common questions we get is, "How many children do we have?" Our response is, "We have four boys, although Darla argues she has five." The question and response suggests possession. Hans, Josh, Lucas, and Logan are our boys. They make up our family.

They are, in other words, my people. They are and we are . . . Vander Plaats. You, your parents, your children, and your relatives are your family. Family is what defines us and what separates us. Thus, names are important.

This is why Solomon says in his search of wisdom and in his writing in the book of Proverbs, chapter 22, verse 1, that "a good name is more desirable than riches; to be esteemed is better than silver or gold." And we as God's people don't bear just any name or only our earthly name. We bear His name.

This is what is so striking about God's response to Solomon in the 2 Chronicles 7:14 verse. God doesn't state that He desires the prayers and the repentance from those who don't bear His name, those who are apart from Him, or those who don't know Him. He clearly states "My people."

As a parent, my children matter most to me. Sure, kids in general are important to me. I even became a teacher and a coach and a high school principal because of my love for children. In fact, my current role serving the interest of the families of Iowa and of the United States is out of my love for children and for future generations.

But, make no mistake, it is my children, my boys, those who are birthed from my bloodline, who are my top priority.

I believe it to be the same with God. He loves all of His creation, we are all His creation, and we all bear His image and likeness. As stated in Genesis 1:26–28,

> *Then God said, "Let us make man in our image, after our likeness. And let them have dominion over the fish of the sea and over the birds of the heavens and over the livestock and over all the earth and over every creeping thing that creeps on the earth." So God created man in his own image, in the image of God he created him; male and female he created them. And God blessed them. And God said to them, "Be fruitful and multiply and fill the earth and subdue it and have dominion over the fish of the sea and over the birds of the heavens and over every living thing that moves on the earth."*

Yes, we are all His creation; however, we are not all His people. And this verse for revival is for . . . "His people."

The more things change the more things stay the same. I remember nagging and begging my parents to cave in on the ridiculous midnight curfew they put in place for me on Friday nights. After stating all the well-thought out manipulations of why I should have my curfew extended to 2 a.m., I reserved the excuse that would surely trump all others . . . surely leading them to embrace my terms: "All of the other parents are letting their kids stay out past midnight."

My dad would typically reply, "Those kids aren't my kids, nor are they my responsibility." And he would add that as long as I lived under his roof and bore his name, my curfew would be midnight. He also would add a valuable insight such as "If all the other kids jump off a high bridge, are you going to jump because they jumped?"

Ironically, my boys have attempted the same strategy with me. And guess what? My reply is pretty much on par with the teaching of my parents.

I never played organized football and don't consider myself a football player. That being said, I always look forward with great anticipation toward Saturdays and Sundays filled with college and NFL football festivities.

I enjoy the game. I really enjoy the fans, because on game days the fans display the flags, wear the jerseys, sing the fight songs, and ready themselves for the Monday morning office victory speeches in honor of their team. In Iowa, these fanatics call themselves Hawkeyes, Cyclones, Panthers, Bulldogs, Raiders, etc. Across the country, they call themselves Vikings, 49ers, Bengals, Cowboys, etc.

These games are big, and it requires everyone's collective best to achieve the desired outcome. And the outcome can make or break a weekend, a week, a season, or a year, depending on one's level of fanaticism.

However, this revival verse isn't talking about our allegiance and loyalty to our favorite football team. It is calling out our belonging and our love for our God. Thus, "My people" refers to God's team.

In the Old Testament, God's people were limited to the Israelites. However, under the New Covenant, it is open to us. John 3:16 states, "God so loved the world that he gave his one and only Son, that whoever believes in him shall not perish but have eternal life."

This saving grace to be on God's team is available to all who confess "Jesus is Lord," and who, because of God's grace, are in right standing before God. God's Word confirms this for us:

We are His people:

But you are a chosen people, a royal priesthood, a holy nation, God's special possession, that you may declare the praises of him who called you out of darkness into his wonderful light. Once you were not a people, but now you are the people of God . . .

1 PETER 2:9–10

John says we are children of God:

Yet to all who did receive him, to those who believed in his name, he gave the right to become children of God.

JOHN 1:12

Jesus calls us His disciples:

To the Jews who believed him, Jesus said, "If you hold to my teaching, you are really my disciples."

John 8:31

"By this everyone will know you are my disciples, if you love one another."

John 13:35

The transition flows from outward to inward:

A person is not a Jew who is one only outwardly, nor is circumcision merely outward and physical. No, a person is a Jew who is one inwardly; and circumcision is circumcision of the heart by the Spirit, not by the written code. Such a person's praise is not from other people, but from God.

Romans 2:28–29

In Sunday school we were taught a song with the lyrics, "Though none go with me, still I will follow." This song reinforced our commitment to being one of God's people, fully knowing the cost of separation from this world by being one of His people. The lyrics flowed easy and the tune was fun to sing. However, the message prepared us for making the commitment to follow Jesus, identifying ourselves as one of God's people.

If you are like me, you'd prefer that revival and responsibility be placed on some distant person or place. This is not the case for those of us on God's team. In football terms, it is the responsibility of the Hawkeyes, not the

Cyclones, for the Iowa Hawks to win a national championship.

In revival terms, it's up to God's people, and it begins with me, with you, with our families, and with our churches. Or in the spirit of the Sunday school song, and in the message from Joshua who instructs us to obey, "As for me and my household, we will serve the LORD" (Joshua 24:15).

We are His people. And, in this verse, God our coach makes our revival role clear. He wants His people to take responsibility.

CHAPTER 3

"WHO ARE CALLED"

. . . for the gifts
and the calling of God
are irrevocable.

ROMANS 11:29 NASB

for the gifts

"Who Are Called"

It's no secret that I love the game of basketball. And as anyone who has ever played organized sports knows, being on the bench, on the sideline, in the dugout, or in the box is an experience that includes very mixed emotions. Before the game, the butterflies, the adrenaline, the nerves, the anticipation, and the prayers seem to mesh together all at once. It's a rush, and thus the thrill and the addiction and the obsession of sport.

If you are like I was in college, one of those who "rides the pine" and waits for your name to be called, these pregame emotions perpetuate with the ebb and flow of the game. To be transparent, when it comes to off the field of play, there are many times when your excitement and anticipation for contribution to the competition can turn into boredom and frustration.

The song that says, "Put me in, Coach . . . I'm ready to play," is a most appropriate theme song for many who've put in, but are not experiencing . . . the time.

While in college, a few of us on the bench decided to have fun at the expense of one another. Not knowing when or if we would get put in, we commenced implementing our own game plan of preplanned pranks to pass the time and to keep one another on an inappropriate edge in case our name was "called" and our talent needed by the coach.

I won't go into all of our planned and failed schemes, but permit me to explain one that was executed to perfection. Our Northwestern Raiders of Iowa were on the road in a nonconference matchup. The key words in the previous sentence are *on the road* and *nonconference.* Typically, these phrases combine to mean our guard was down.

Our team's guard may have been down and our intensity lacking, but Coach's guard was up and his intensity was growing in response to our team's lethargic play. Those of us on the bench could sense the tension and anticipated our name being called with the hope of inserting some life and urgency into our play, with the goal of turning the game in our favor.

These dynamics became the perfect storm for a "seemed like a good idea at the time" plan that should have never been executed by my cohort, BJ, and me. However, through whispers and snickers and premeditated adrenalin, we indeed executed it flawlessly. BJ was to my left and Scott was to my right. BJ turned to me and said, "Plaats, tell Scott that Coach wants him in." I turned to an unassuming Scott and said, "Scott, Coach wants you in." Scott replied in disbelief and in a bit of shock said, "What?" BJ and I both turned to Scott at once and in unison said, "Scott, NOW! Coach wants you in!"

Scott leapt from the bench and, as we all did for drama and affect, thrust off his breakaway pants and tore off his shooting shirt while scurrying to Coach's side. Coach happened to be off the bench and turned away yelling "inspiration" to our team and "correction" to the officials. Coach was animated and not happy. However, this was just the beginning.

When Coach spun on his bench-scuffed dress shoes to follow the play on the other end of the court, Scott was standing in the perfect substitution posture. Coach's spin just about knocked Scott over as he was bouncing to his toes, his heart racing, in full anticipation of being inserted into the game. A stunned and not amused Coach glared into Scott's eyes and expressed through great frustration, "What are you doing here?" Scott blushed and almost fainted as he stuttered, "I thought you called my name."

Coach wasted no time in making it clear to Scott that he had not called his name, and that he should return to his place on the bench immediately. As Scott returned to his seat, BJ and I were an emotional mess. We hid our faces in our shooting shirts to conceal our out-of-control laughter, as our bodies almost shook our lungs into hyperventilation.

As Scott passed by, he assured us that our certain demise was close at hand. Quite frankly, we didn't care. The precision and timing of our scheming was executed flawlessly, and our entire bench's laughter, including the assistant coach, was our reward.

As we celebrated our little victory and laughed when Coach wasn't looking our way, we also expressed exuberant inspiration to our team in an effort to redirect uncontrollable emotions when Coach looked our direction. Although we hadn't played one second of the contest, we were exhausted.

In the midst of all this, Coach legitimately did call BJ's name. Not surprisingly, BJ's focus wasn't on Coach, so he didn't hear his name. Other team members immediately turned to BJ and relayed Coach's call for BJ, whose response through laughter was, "Unh, unh . . . nice try. . . . I'm not falling for that!" Just then Coach raced over to BJ and grabbed him by the shooting shirt, flinging him to the scorer's bench.

Through it all, we lost the game. Our team didn't play well. BJ didn't play well. Scott didn't play well. And I didn't play well. However, it remains an unforgettable memory.

I share all of this to illustrate the authenticity of the "Call." Our call to Scott was not authentic and surely disingenuous. Coach's call to BJ, much to BJ's surprise, was authentic.

In a very odd way, this story reminds me of the call God places to the child Samuel in the Old Testament (1 Samuel 1—3). As a reminder, Samuel was dedicated to God and given over to Eli, the High Priest at the temple, as a thanksgiving offering by Samuel's parents.

Samuel retires in the temple for the evening and hears a voice calling his name, "Samuel." He races to Eli's side, inquiring what Eli needs of him. Eli tells the boy he did not call him and to go back to bed. Again, Samuel hears his name. Again, Samuel rushes to see what Eli needs. Again, Eli summons Samuel back to his quarters.

It happens once again. However, this time Eli summarizes that Samuel's call is from God Himself. Eli tells young Samuel to go back to bed and the next time he hears this voice and call, he should say, "Here I am, Lord; your servant is listening."

God speaks to Samuel.

The recounting of this famous Old Testament story gives clarity to Samuel's "Call" from God. Most Christians I know pray that God will make their "Call" from Him equally as clear.

This part of the revival verse strikes to our inner core and most deeply held need: "God's Call." Are we truly "Called"? After all, Scripture is clear that the Israelites for whom this revival verse was intended were indeed God's chosen people. They were obviously "Called."

However, are you "Called"? Am I "Called"? If we claim His name through His Son, Jesus Christ, then I say yes, God is calling you. He wants His relationship with His followers to be authentic. As the apostle James says, "Faith without works is dead."

Better yet, as Christ says in His parting in Matthew with the Great Commission, read Matthew 28:16–20 slowly,

> *Then the eleven disciples went to Galilee, to the mountain where Jesus had told them to go. When they saw him, they worshiped him; but some doubted. Then Jesus came to them and said, "All authority in heaven and on earth has been given to me. Therefore go and make disciples of all nations, baptizing*

them in the name of the Father and of the Son and of the Holy Spirit, and teaching them to obey everything I have commanded you. And surely I am with you always, to the very end of the age."

Talk about mission statements! This one has it all and should be used as the model for all subsequent missions. First, Jesus makes it clear that He has given this authority. This should be the Alpha and the Omega of the authority flowchart.

Second, He tells them to "go!" I love this because "go" is laced with action. Jesus obviously has no need to mince words. He wants, desires, and needs action from His disciples. Then He follows one action word immediately with another—"make." The modern-day translation instilled in me by my dad, my teachers, my coaches, and my mentors is: Don't just "go," but do something or "make!"

And what does He want His disciples to make? He wants His disciples to make more disciples. Jesus is in the multiplication business, which He knows is the exponential factor in bringing those apart from Him to Him. The best news is Jesus makes this available to all, not just to some or a few.

Get ready, because here comes another action word for the disciples—"baptizing." Baptism is the outward sign of a new life and a new identity. Jesus says baptize them in the name of the Father, of the Son, and of the Holy Spirit. Those who accept this free gift and take on this new identity are now "Called."

Applying the Great Commission is two-thirds sanctification and one-third salvation. Arguably, the salvation part is most crucial. But make no mistake, Christ applies the bookends of discipleship with another action word, "teaching," to emphasize the Father's heart for action.

Yes, it is you, and it is me, whom He "Calls." Thus, we have to stop the finger-pointing. Revival starts with His people whom He has called. So for us Christians, the "Who Are Called" is us. For you Christian, the "Who Are Called" is you. And for me, it is me.

Ultimately, revival is God's responsibility. That being said, it is clear that God wants us . . . all of us—all of our heart, all of our soul, all of our mind, and all of our strength.

CHAPTER 4

"BY MY NAME"

O my God, incline Your ear and hear!
Open Your eyes and see our desolations
and the city which is called by Your name;
for we are not presenting our supplications
before You on account of any merits of our own,
but on account of Your great compassion.

DANIEL 9:18 NASB

"By My Name"

At the age of thirteen, my dad felt as though his name was removed from him.

On July 15, 1939, Dad (age thirteen) had the task of finishing chores on the family farm. His younger brother, Harold (age twelve), was given the duty of caring for their one-year-old sister, Myrna, while their parents and brothers Wilton and Gerrit went to town to sell eggs and purchase food and goods in preparation for the Sabbath.

It was a beautiful summer day in Sheldon, Iowa, when my dad's father, Arie Vander Plaats, gathered sons Wilton and Gerrit and wife, Sadie, to accompany him on the weekly journey from their rural farm to the town of Sheldon.

No one knows why, but while Dad was tending to chores and Harold was tending to Myrna and the home, their dad, Arie, exited the driveway into the path of an oncoming vehicle. A loud crash was heard . . . cars were spun . . . lives were changed.

Dad immediately ran to the scene and witnessed first-hand the aftermath of the crash that would race him into adulthood. Arie was hanging on by a thin thread as was evident by his unconscious state and swaying head. Wilton was flung from the front seat and pinned under the car's left front tire. Gerrit suffered severe injuries to his head, eye, nose, and jaw and was unconscious in the backseat. Sadie was in obvious shock and instructed my dad to run to the neighbors, the Postmas, to summon help.

The hearse, which also served as the ambulance in those days, arrived on the scene. Concerned helpers loaded Arie, Wilton, and Gerrit into the hearse. Sadie walked herself to the hearse. Dad and Harold could only sit, think, pray, and think some more about the future as they sat inside the Postma's home.

The initial news came from their pastor, Reverend Byema. Upon entering the Postma home, Reverend Byema informed them that Sadie had passed away approximately thirty minutes after arriving at the hospital, having suffered injuries to her back and chest. The news that she had died came as a shock, since she was able to walk herself to the vehicle for transport to the hospital . . . and that is what most believe, including my dad, killed her—shock.

As Dad and Harold adjourned to bed for the evening, reality had set in. They would not sleep. They sat up and discussed the events of the day. They were devastated and extremely unsure about their future. Their thoughts ranged from why, to how, to what, to when, to where, and back to why again.

The next day brought more bad news. Wilton had died at 8:30 p.m. on Saturday, and Arie passed on at 5:30 Sunday morning. Gerrit remained in the hospital for months before recovering enough from his injuries to return home.

After absorbing the catastrophic news, twelve-year-old Harold and thirteen-year-old Dad made a pact. They were going to remain Vander Plaats. Thus, adoption was out of the question. And if anyone attempted to put them in an orphanage, they would run away. They lost a mom, a dad, and a brother, but they didn't lose a sense of family. And I lost grandparents whom I never knew. They defined their attitude early on in the midst of tragedy. They were family. They were going to make it through this . . . together . . . as Vander Plaats. They were determined to hold on to their name as they held on to each other.

From early on, names are important.

Ponder the following names: Barak Obama, Bill Clinton, Saddam Hussein, George Bush, Princess Diana, Michael Jordan, Lincoln, Sinatra, Donald Trump, Chuck Norris, Ronald Reagan, Cosby, Margaret Thatcher, Tiger, Muhammad Ali, Vince Lombardi, Bach, Beethoven, Martin Luther, Michael Jackson, Whitney Houston, Kennedy, Marilyn Monroe, Hitler, The Beatles, Billy Graham, and Jesus.

Each name conjures a memory or, at minimum, an impression. This is why businesses, politicians, musicians, authors, churches, nonprofit organizations, and the Kardashians spend hundreds and thousands and millions and billions of dollars to saturate the market with a desired impression to go with their name. Names are important.

As stated in the previous chapter, Solomon tells us,

> *A good name is more desirable than riches; to be esteemed is better than silver or gold.*

From a human perspective, we too often mistake a good name for a better name or for a best name. Thus, we compete to elevate our name, our presence, and our standing above others. If this is you or your company, take heart, it's not just the twenty-first-century egos; it occurred with Jesus' disciples as well.

The story is recounted for us in the Gospel of Mark. Jesus and His disciples were on their way to Capernaum, and there was some arguing or modern-day "trash talking" going on among Jesus' followers. When they got in the house, Jesus asked the disciples, "What were you arguing about on the road?" Jesus knew what they were bickering about but saw a teachable moment for His apprentices.

The disciples remained quiet out of shame for their conduct and posturing. Jesus then seized the awkward quiet and instructed on how to be the greatest. He said to the twelve, "Anyone who wants to be first must be the very last, and the servant of all" (Mark 9:35). Talk about turning the world on its proverbial head! If you want to be first, you must become last; if you want to be great, you must be the least, and if you are to be a leader, you must become a servant. Now that's a model for leadership.

However, Jesus doesn't stop by just turning the world's measure of greatness philosophy upside down; He finishes His comments with the importance of His name. As the story is told, Jesus takes a child into His arms to illustrate an object lesson for His class . . . His disciples . . . His followers . . . for you and for me.

As He embraces this child, He commences the lesson: "Whoever welcomes one of these little children in my name welcomes me; and whoever welcomes me does not welcome me but the one who sent me" (Mark 9:37). The message is powerful and clear. His desire is for us to welcome, nurture, train, and love children in "His name." And, by the way, God is the greatest.

As I write about Jesus instructing His disciples concerning who is the greatest, I reflect on the lyrics of the song "Above All" by Michael W. Smith. Read these words. Listen to these words. Play these words. Sing these words. Remember these words:

> *Above all powers, above all kings, above all nature and all created things. Above all wisdom and all the ways of man, You were here before the world began. Above all kingdoms, above all thrones, above all wonders the world has ever known, above all wealth and treasures of the earth, there is no way to measure what You are worth.*

God the Father . . . the Alpha and Omega (the Beginning and the End) . . . Yahweh (I Am) . . . Adonai (the Lord, my great Lord) . . . Elohim (the All-Powerful One, Creator) . . . El Roi (the God who sees me) . . . El Shaddai (the All-Sufficient One) . . . Immanuel (God with us) . . . Jehovah . . . I AM . . . God is the greatest!

And God takes His great name seriously. Remember as He chooses Moses to lead the Israelites out of captivity,

Moses asks a very real question in Exodus 3, beginning at verse 13. Moses said to God, "Suppose I go to the Israelites and say to them, 'The God of your fathers has sent me to you,' and they ask me, 'What is his name?' Then, what shall I tell them?"

God tells Moses to keep it simple and tell them, "I AM WHO I AM. Tell them I AM has sent me to you." "I AM," meaning there is "no other" . . . period.

God tells Moses to explain it to them by telling them, "The LORD, the God of your fathers—the God of Abraham, the God of Isaac and the God of Jacob—has sent me to you. 'This is my name forever, the name you shall call me from generation to generation.'"

Therefore, it is no surprise God begins the Ten Commandments given to Moses on Mount Sinai with a clear reminder of who He is and the importance of His name. As recorded for us in Exodus 20:1–6:

> *I am the LORD your God, who brought you out of Egypt, out of the land of slavery. You shall have no other gods before me. You shall not make for yourself an image in the form of anything in heaven above or the earth beneath or in the waters below. You shall not bow down to them or worship them; for I, the LORD your God, am a jealous God, punishing the children for the sin of the parents to the third and fourth generation of those who hate me, but showing love to a thousand generations of those who love me and keep my commandments.*

And now for the exclamation point in verse 7,

You shall not misuse the name of the LORD your God, for the LORD will not hold anyone guiltless who misuses His name.

I believe He wants us to understand the importance of His name. His name is higher than any other name. No other names should ever be elevated above His name anywhere, anyplace, or anytime. And watch out if you choose to undermine, degrade, or misuse His name.

I believe it would be wise to highlight this portion of the Ten Commandments as it relates to God's name prior to every sporting event. God's name is reserved for our eternal reverence not our earthly rage.

When God states "My name" in this verse for revival, He elevates the importance and seriousness to the highest degree . . . His name!

CHAPTER 5

"WILL HUMBLE THEMSELVES"

A true revival means nothing less
than a revolution,
casting out the spirit of worldliness
and selfishness,
and making God and His love
triumph in the heart and life.

Andrew Murray

true revival

"Will Humble Themselves"

In a manner of full disclosure, this chapter is proving to be the most difficult to write. I'd much rather write about "If," "My People," "Who Are Called," and "By My Name." Humility doesn't come easy for me. And, the oddity of that comment is, I have so little about which to be boastful or prideful.

Typically, we are humble after we are humiliated. In sports, we trash talk the opponent until the scoreboard takes the trash out of our talk. In politics, we boast of our sure victories until the voting population sides with our opponent. In church, we build buildings and trumpet numbers until we can't sustain our budget. In fact, I heard one pastor referencing the movie *Field of Dreams*, when he said that instead of the famed movie quote, "If you build it, they will come," in the church world the quote would read, "If you build it, they must come."

Let's take a look at a few famous people who have been

caught in a sin or transgression, where humility via personal humiliation surely follows. Tiger Woods humbles himself by taking time off from golf in order to get a grip on his life, after his wife exposes him for adulterous behavior. Famed football quarterback Michael Vick holds a news conference expressing how he has come to Jesus after he is arrested for organized gambling involving high stakes dogfights.

My experience tells me these humble transitions are not limited to high profile figures displayed in the media. You and I do the same. When we are young, we feel ok and even somewhat accomplished for taking the forbidden cookies. However, when Mom discovers our hand in the cookie jar, we quickly humble ourself, seeking mercy. We believe our driving performance is the envy of NASCAR until the red lights of the state patrol pull us over to visit about our violation.

I chalk the above up to our sinful nature, giving validity to this nature as expressed in the first words out of a toddler's mouth . . . "mine!" As we grow older, our desire is for "more" of "mine." I want more pay. I deserve a better position. I envy more possessions. And the list goes on to satisfy our self-focused desires.

God knows our self-absorbed nature all too well. That's why He instructs us to humble or take the focus off of ourselves. C. S. Lewis illustrates the definition of humility as not thinking less of yourself, but rather thinking of yourself less.

Think of all the trouble we get ourselves into when we are prideful and self-focused. We may not say it audibly, but our actions speak that we are "god." Yes, we pay lip service, because that is expected. But as long as the ship is floating smoothly, our attitude is that "we are in charge." When we hit the iceberg, we reach out to God. Last time I checked, this violates Commandments One through Four and gives credence to the oft-stated proverb, "Pride goes before the fall."

As a matter of fact, all the Ten Commandments are up for grabs when the crosshairs are focused on ourselves. Disregarding the teaching of Mom and Dad and usurping God's given authority is for self. Not observing a Sabbath day to fully focus on our Creator God is due to our obsession with self. Committing adultery is surely a selfish lust. Taking what isn't ours, or stealing, is for self. Bearing false witness or lying is to protect ourselves. Murder ranks as the ultimate selfish act, expunging a life God created for our own revenge, our own convenience, or our own power. And the Tenth Commandment is to provide an all-encompassing guardrail against self—don't covet anything that isn't yours. These commands are so simple, and yet are so personally penetrating.

The more I read these basic commands, the more I realize that these are all designed to keep our "self" in check, which requires humility. Humility puts God first as we honor our parents and keep His Sabbath. Humility checks our selfish lust against desires that are dishonest and harmful to ourselves as well as to others.

The apostle Paul talks about this transparently when he states that he must die to himself daily (1 Corinthians 15:31).

Why? Because he dies to himself in proper alignment to God, to God's call on his life, in order to be of service to others. If he doesn't die to himself, his selfish desires and focus grow, and God's purpose for his life spins out of control.

As mentioned in the previous chapter, my dad is a veteran of World War II. The men and women of this period in history are frequently, and accurately, depicted by many as "the Greatest Generation." What made this generation so great is that they embraced a spirit of putting the cause of others above themselves. And this spirit didn't end with the culmination of the World War II victory and service to country. The Greatest Generation passed this spirit of humility on to their families, to their churches, to their communities, and to their country. In other words, they took the focus off of themselves in humility, and the result . . . greatness!

Ironic, isn't it, that when you put others first, causes first, and most importantly God first, and yourself last, you are regarded as great? It seems we are pushed and encouraged and judged by our personal elevation and success. Yet we find true greatness when, as Paul, we die to ourselves . . . we humble ourselves.

Jesus set the bar during the Last Supper in the upper room with His disciples. The Scriptures relay to us in John 13 that after the Passover feast, Jesus knew His time had come to return to the Father. So what does He do? He removes His clothes and puts a towel around His waist and begins to wash and dry His disciples' feet. In recognizing Jesus, Master and Lord and Messiah, washing the dirty road-traveled feet,

Peter objects. Jesus tells Peter that he doesn't realize yet what He is doing but soon he will understand.

Jesus was providing them a glimpse into the "full extent" of His love for them. Jesus, name above all names, is humbling Himself by washing His disciples' feet. After He finished washing their feet, this is what He says to them in John 13:12–17:

> *"Do you understand what I have done for you?" he asked them. "You call me 'Teacher' and 'Lord,' and rightly so, for that is what I am. Now that I, your Lord and Teacher, have washed your feet, you also should wash one another's feet. I have set an example that you should do as I have done for you. Very truly I tell you, no servant is greater than his master, nor is a messenger greater than the one who sent him. Now that you know these things, you will be blessed if you do them."*

There is no greater example of humility than the Savior of all, stripping Himself down to a towel and washing the feet of His disciples. And see what He emphasizes in His teaching to them? That they will be blessed . . . we will be blessed . . . if we follow His example!

This teaching and leading by example blows our modern-day thinking and teaching out of the proverbial water. We are taught from early on that this life is about us. It is about success and rungs on a ladder. It is about accumulation, and the one who dies with the most toys wins. Every commercial tells us how to look better, drive better, live better, and reinforces the belief that this life is about us.

But Jesus says, "No, it's not." God says in this revival verse, "Humble yourselves." Or in other words, take the focus off yourself and place it on God. Stop the perpetual madness of attempting to please your flesh with the things of this world that will never satisfy, and instead pursue God and His righteousness. Jesus rocks our worldview as He sums up this teaching in Matthew 6:33 when He says,

> *"But seek first his kingdom and his righteousness, and all these things will be given to you as well."*

What are "all these things"? I believe these are the desires of our earthly pursuits . . . fulfillment, purpose, and satisfaction. But notice the order: seek God and His righteousness . . . then . . . and not before . . .

Darla and I are blessed to have four boys. Our third son, Lucas, is uniquely crafted and gifted. He cannot walk or talk. He breathes through the surgical implant of a tracheotomy, eats his food through a g-tube, and his back is held straight via a full spinal fusion procedure. Due to his very rare brain disorder, he encounters many mini to mega seizures that can alter his day, placing him on the edge between continued life or earthly death at all times.

Most onlookers recognize his earthly limitations and feel sorry for him because he's obviously not "normal." Yet there are many times when I believe Lucas must feel sorry for us. You see, he's not caught up in the game of personal elevation and make-believe appearances. He is who he is, and his authenticity and focus on others draws our family and others to him.

In his book, *Light from Lucas,* I tell the reader that Lucas has delivered the most powerful sermon on how to live life without ever uttering a word. Lucas's life offers those of us who are "normal" the opportunity to transition our thinking from "I'm entitled" to "I'm blessed." I get to run. I get to eat. I get to drive. I get to serve. I get to . . . Many times when I get my focus distorted, Darla will tell me to take Lucas for a walk. What she is not so casually insinuating is that I need to transition my thinking from entitlement to blessing . . . from focus on self to focus on others . . . from personal obsession to humility.

If you struggle, as I do, with this focus from time to time, I suggest you visit Lucas. And if not Lucas, visit Wendy. Wendy is a special friend of ours who has Down's syndrome. She'll not only smile when she greets you, she'll offer you an "I love you" hug. She won't only smile and hug, she'll laugh at your jokes, and she'll express a heartfelt "ahh" if you've experienced a disappointment.

I believe God places these special gifts, such as Lucas and Wendy and others, in our lives to teach us about our frailty and the proper focus and alignment in our lives.

Simply put . . . God is God . . . we are not . . . and He desires our humility.

CHAPTER 6

"AND PRAY"

There is a moral and spiritual war
for the souls of Americans.
And this war must be waged
by preaching the Gospel, prayer,
and obedience to God's Word.

DAVID JEREMIAH

"And Pray"

I went to be a blessing.

A friend and longtime pastor who just announced his retirement fell victim to a massive brain bleed. From every angle, it was a bad deal happening to a great man.

As he was receiving medical care at a major hospital in the region, Darla and I decided to pay him a visit. Since we were out for a cruise with Lucas, we took Lucas along. This is significant because Lucas despises hospitals. He has had his share of life flights, emergency rooms, and ICUs to last him a lifetime. The very scent of a medical facility puts him into a less than desirable mood.

However, on this Sunday in Pastor Gary's hospital room, Lucas was alert and engaged, not appearing agitated in the least. It was unusual enough that when Darla and I left the room, we asked each other, "What's the deal with Lucas?"

Gary and his wife seemed to welcome the company. We had a great conversation, but in an effort not to tire him, we left after about fifteen minutes. Gary's audible voice had been reduced to a faint whisper, and it took much energy to understand his comments. As we were exiting the room, I shook his hand and expressed that we would keep him in our prayers. He immediately stiffened his grip on my hand and didn't let go as his gaze pierced into my eyes.

Then through a faint whisper he said, "Will you really?" Taken back a bit by his question, I replied that I would. He then asked again. I reassured him, once again, that we would. It was at this moment that the preacher, via a faint whisper, delivered the sermon.

He quickly and emphatically stated that the words, *I'll pray for you*, can be hollow and not really meant. He, as a believer and as a teacher of the Word, embraced the power of prayer. Thus, he didn't want it to be said casually and without meaning. He wanted us to truly commit to pray for him, for his wife, for his family, and for God's perfect will.

Pastor Gary realized what God knows all too well. Our words committing ourselves to prayer are many times void and shallow. Gary wanted me to mean it. I believe, in this revival verse, God wants us to mean it as well.

As Darla and I resumed our Sunday cruise in our family Suburban with Lucas, we discussed the visit with Pastor Gary and his wife in great detail. We quickly summarized that we may have gone to visit Gary to be a blessing, but, true to form, we left feeling as though we were the ones who were blessed.

I don't believe it is any accident that the words *and pray* follow the words *will humble*. Praying, in and of itself, is a measure and natural result of true humility. When we pray, we recognize that there is a God . . . it is not us . . . and we are completely dependent on Him.

Praying also indicates our desire to have a relationship with our Creator. Many wives have ended up dismissing their spouses due to the husband's reluctance to communicate. God, similar to the wife who wants to bond with her husband, wants a relationship with us. He desires our praise and adoration. He desires to hear our deepest needs and concerns. He desires for us to acknowledge Him for our provision. And He wants to hear us say, "It's up to You, not me."

Jesus teaches about prayer during His Sermon on the Mount recorded for us by Matthew in chapter 6. And the net of Jesus' teaching is authenticity. He warns us against praying just to be seen or just to be heard. Instead, He advises us to go to the Father in secret . . . one-on-one with the door closed.

I believe He recommends this because this act reduces the distractions and increases the intimacy, the focus, and the authenticity. In other words, Jesus is saying it is a measure of our hearts. And when the Father sees what is done in secret . . . not for the recognition of others . . . we will receive His reward.

It is difficult for me to comprehend that the Creator of the universe cares enough for me and loves me to this degree that He desires a deep relationship. He wants, and His Word consistently commands, us to pray.

Jesus continues by telling us not to babble like the pagans, for they think they will be heard for their many words. We've all been in conversations with other people where we leave exhausted and we didn't even utter a word. It's as though we want to yell, "I got it . . . " but due to some misguided etiquette, we stand and we absorb and deflect word after word.

Jesus recommends instead of babbling that we keep our prayers focused. He reassures us by stating that the Father already knows what we need even before we utter a word.

The disciples who traveled along with Jesus desired this intimacy with the One who sent the Son. As recorded in Luke 11, Jesus was off by himself praying, and when He finished, one of the disciples asked Him to teach them how to pray. And what's really cool, Jesus taught them.

What I mean by that is that He didn't just say, "Well, you just start talking to God and tell Him what's on your heart." Not that this approach would be wrong, but it would have skipped the needed discipline, structure, and focus of prayer. I believe this casual approach would have diluted the measured and intentional importance of communicating with our Creator.

I used to coach basketball. As a coach, it would be negligent for me to merely throw the ball on the court and say to the aspiring player, "Go play." Instead, coaches go through painstaking measures of repetition, teaching the fundamentals of the game. From ball-handling drills, to defensive stance and posture, to rebounding technique, to forward and reverse pivots, and form shooting . . . good coaches are insistent on teaching the fundamentals.

The goal is for these fundamentals to become second nature or habits of play. This is why fundamentals are taught and reinforced from little league, to middle school, to high school, to college, and throughout professional careers. Fundamentals of the game matter, so they need to be taught, repeated, and constantly reinforced. Not even a great athlete such as Michael Jordan would have become the championship and Hall of Fame player without learning and honing the fundamentals throughout his career.

I encourage all readers to critically research the continuum of play of Michael Jordan from high school, to college, to his sixth championship with the Chicago Bulls. The results clearly show a much refined ball handler, passer, shooter, penetrator, and rebounder. These results came about because of attention to and repetition of the fundamentals.

The same is true with prayer. My guess is, if you are anything like me, that your prayer life can use some attention to the fundamentals.

Jesus understood this, so when asked by His disciples on how to pray, He provided a structure that focused on the fundamentals of prayer. I know we're talking about Jesus, but the simplicity is flat-out brilliant!

Let's break it down together . . .

Our Father

Jesus begins with an attention grabber . . . "Our Father." Immediately, Jesus provides close proximity to the perceived distant. Our God is our Creator, and it's natural to perceive Him to be "out there" somewhere. Jesus breaks this paradigm by instructing us to call Him, "Father."

Most of us can relate to earthly fathers or, at minimum, father figures. Dads are important. They provide, they love, they care, they protect, they encourage, and they provide stability. Well, at least that's the design.

I'm fortunate . . . I had a good dad. And although he would be the first to admit that he wasn't perfect, he strived to do all of the above. It was always comforting to know that I had someone I could call if I was in need. My dad passed away nearly four years ago, and there is hardly a day that goes by that I don't think about him . . . about what he would say . . . what he would recommend . . . what update he would like to hear . . . what would make him laugh. Many times I still catch myself desiring to press his speed dial number in my phone, thinking I should call him.

I'm doubly blessed because Darla's dad is one these dads who, too, desires the best for his children. Although his approach is different than my dad's, it's comforting to know that he is there for us if we need him.

I hope you have had a similar experience with your dad. However, even if your earthly father didn't live up to these fatherhood pillars, be assured your heavenly Father does. He wants the best for you, and that's why Jesus shatters the distant paradigm of prayer by instructing us to call Him . . . "Father." Wow!

Who Art in Heaven

My profession requires me to be on calls with people all over the country and, at times, internationally. One thing I always enjoy is the opportunity to travel to meet the person I've been visiting with by phone on their own turf. It completely changes my imagery the next time I call. I can place the voice with a face and with their surroundings.

Jesus does this when He gives us the location of the Father. He is in heaven, seated on His throne, listening to my prayer, to your prayer, to our corporate prayers.

Hallowed Be Your Name

There it is again . . . His name. The angels cried out in Isaiah 6, "Holy, holy, holy is the LORD God Almighty!" What a privilege that we get to approach a perfect Father, whose name is above all names, above all kings, above all kingdoms. This provides the perspective and the reverence in our approach.

I remember the first time Darla and I and two of our four boys, Logan and Josh, were able to meet the president of the United States. We dressed appropriately and were on time for our meeting with the president. After going through security and waiting patiently in line, we had our few anxious minutes and a photo with the sitting president, George W. Bush. This remains a special memory.

No disrespect intended for President Bush, but consider the open invitation we have as believers to approach the throne of God, our Father, in heaven. It should blow our minds that He desires this communication on a frequent basis with us, His children. This isn't an earthly president or king; this is the King of kings!

Your Kingdom Come

When we encounter the one true living God, nothing and no one else will do. This is where Scripture in 2 Corinthians 5:17 says, "The old has gone, the new is here!" This transformation assures that this life, this body, this career, this circumstance, and this world is not the end. There is so much more.

Jesus knew this full well as He descended from glory to walk with and to teach us here on earth. Yes, "Your Kingdom Come" is a passionate prayer from God's people.

Your Will Be Done on Earth As It Is in Heaven

I believe this portion of the prayer has to do with order. In this earthly world, we are surrounded by chaos, by sickness and disease, by death, by torn relationships, by selfish wants and desires, by lies, by natural disasters, by brokenness, and by a plethora of consequences due to our sinful nature.

In heaven, we get a glimpse of order. God is seated on His throne with His Son, Jesus, seated at His right hand. We are told of streets of gold and seas of crystal. Heaven is filled with love, with beauty, with truth, and with praises in perfect harmony.

Yes, we should desire God, His truth, His righteousness, and His love on earth as it certainly is in heaven.

Give Us This Day Our Daily Bread

As a former educator, I believe it is a mistake that we stripped prayer from the public schools; specifically, as it relates to teachers casually dismissing their students to lunch. I believe it is better to remind children that it is not the school, nor the government, nor even their parents who are providing for this basic human need. Instead, God Himself is our Provider.

This portion of the prayer is about provision. It is about recognizing our dependence on God for such basic needs as food, health, clothing, and shelter. The home we live in, the car(s) we drive, the five-star restaurants we frequent, and our fashion-designer wardrobes are all a gift from God. It is only the fool who believes it is of his own effort.

***Free editorial: The "entitlement" mentality of our children and of our society begins with feeding millions of school-age youngsters with no acknowledgment of a Provider.

And Forgive Us Our Debts (Our Trespasses)

Here we repent of our sinful nature, the tangible sin in our life that separates us from God, and fully recognize our need for a Savior.

When a person puts their faith in Jesus, God wipes away all their sins of the past. Sin breaks the fellowship of man with God. Following salvation, the pursuit is to live a sanctified life. Although on this side of eternity we will live with sin and its consequences, the desire is to live our lives submitted to the pursuit of God's holiness, which keeps us in communion with him.

As We Forgive Our Debtors
(Those Who Trespass Against Us)

Jesus reminds us that as we have been forgiven much, we need to forgive much. We all fall short on this side of eternity. Thus, there is a great need for grace from a loving God and from His people.

When Peter asks Jesus in Matthew 18:21, "How many times shall I forgive my brother or sister who sins against me? Up to seven times?" Jesus replies, "I tell you, not seven times, but seventy-seven times."

Jesus obviously knows how far short we fall, and the plethora of opportunities we have to forgive one another. True love is in God, who is willing to forgive, and is reflected with the exponential factor in the forgiven's forgiveness.

And Lead Us Not into Temptation, but Deliver Us from Evil

James 4:7 instructs, "Submit yourselves, then, to God. Resist the devil, and he will flee from you." People of God know that just because we are His and He is ours, Satan does not leave us alone. In fact, it is quite the opposite. Satan wants to destroy our relationship with God and separate us from His love, so he prowls around like a roaring lion, waiting to devour, deceive, and drive us toward our sinful nature.

Jesus, as exampled by His time in the garden of Gethsemane, illustrates this by placing our focus on God and stomping out the power of the devil.

God calls us to pray. In 1 Thessalonians, Paul encourages us to pray without ceasing. Jesus through the Lord's Prayer models for us a template for prayer. In this book and with this "If 7:14 Initiative," we are humbly encouraging God's people to structure their business with quiet times for prayer.

May we honor God with our time, with our humility, with our authenticity . . . with our prayers!

CHAPTER 7

"AND SEEK MY FACE"

Sow with a view to righteousness,
Reap in accordance with kindness;
Break up your fallow ground,
For it is time to seek the LORD
Until He comes to rain righteousness on you.

HOSEA 10:12 NASB

Sow with

CHAPTER 7

"And Seek My Face"

Jesus calls us to get alone with God, to go one-on-one with our Father in heaven. He models a prayer teaching us how to communicate with our Creator. And in this revival verse, God instructs us to "Seek His Face."

Leaders understand the importance of the eyes as it relates to clear, unmistakable communication. Teachers, coaches, and leaders of all stripes are fond of saying, "Look me in the eyes," when communicating needed importance. I believe this is what God is saying to us, His children who bear His name, when He tells us to "Seek His Face." He wants us to look into His eyes, His heart, His character, His love, and His desire.

Can you remember a time when you really sought God's face? If you're anything like me, it was most likely at a time when you were out of all other options . . . when you had nowhere else to turn . . . when you were at the end of yourself. We tend to seek God's face when we can't find our child in the crowd, when the doctor relays an unfavorable health report, and when the sirens blare for one of our loved ones.

I believe it is safe to say that we tend to seek God's face when something important is at stake. It is the urgent situation when nothing less will do.

My first such experience of this came when I was sixteen years old. One hot July night, after cruising the streets of our small town in my '67 Buick Skylark, I managed to arrive home right at midnight . . . just in time to meet my Friday night curfew.

Brian, my older brother, was already asleep in the room we shared and had our window propped open, hoping for a cool breeze. I slipped into bed and was just dozing off when I heard a car speed into our driveway. The front door flew open, then quickly slammed shut as our oldest married brother, Stan, ran up the stairs and down the hall to our parents' bedroom. He spoke with great intensity as he told them to wake up and get dressed, explaining that their fourth-oldest child, Harlan, a.k.a. Hawk, had been severely injured in a car crash. We needed to get to Sioux Falls, South Dakota, as quickly as possible.

The terror still resonates in my mind today when I force myself to remember the details of those early morning moments. I climbed into the family car with my mom and dad and brother Brian. Stan arranged for Vern, a family friend, to drive the seventy-mile journey for us. It was a quiet ride. My mom was stunned silent, only voicing a few deep sighs and an occasional cry of "why" in prayer.

My dad was the man. Clearly, he was concerned about

the condition of his son, but he remained remarkably composed; a source of strength for the rest of us. Little did I know that his example would prove to be so precious when I faced the fear of losing my own son years later. Dad asked Vern to give him the details of the situation. How did it happen? Who was involved? How are the others doing?

The answers made us all aware of the seriousness of the accident. Harlan's girlfriend and the other female passenger were taken to a local hospital, and both were expected to make full recoveries. Vern went on to explain that Dennis, the driver of the car, was "no longer with us." Dennis and Harlan had both been on the driver's side of the vehicle, which absorbed the fatal blow of the collision. The statement, "He's no longer with us," rendered all other details of the accident insignificant. All we were told about Harlan was that he was found unresponsive at the scene, but still breathing on his own. He was in trouble.

When we finally arrived at the hospital, our family gathered in the Intensive Care waiting area. We didn't know what to think or how to act. The doctor finally arrived to inform us that there was little hope for recovery of any kind. Harlan's brain stem looked as if it had been cut with a knife due to the whiplash force of the impact. He was holding on by a very thin thread.

I remember more than any time prior seeking God's face. My prayer begged for mercy, for healing, and for restoration. I wanted my brother to live and return to us the same way he left our home just hours earlier.

Harlan hung on by that thread for five days. Our family

rode the waves from hope to despair. Our prayers coincided with these shifting emotions ranging from "Please allow him to live" to "Please take him peacefully." The waiting area became our home after the accident, and on the fifth day our entire family was called to be by Harlan's bedside.

The timing of this request seemed ironic, since it came almost immediately after Mom and Dad had returned to the waiting area with renewed hope and optimism. You see, each night they would go together, just the two of them, to seek God's face as they prayed at Harlan's bedside. Mom would hold his hand as Dad prayed for divine intervention and for God's will to be done. On this night, Harlan squeezed Mom's hand and pulled it over his heart. What we had interpreted as cause for optimism was actually his way of affirming his love and . . . saying good-bye.

Nevertheless, when the nurses suggested that the family should gather in his room, we did not question them. We moved quickly to his hospital bed, working our way around monitors and life-support equipment. Our family held hands as my oldest brother sought God's face as he offered a prayer on behalf of Hawk and our family.

When he ended his prayer with "Amen," the repetitive beeping of the heart monitor became a single tone, and the screen revealed a straight line. It was a moment of comfort I will always hold dear, for at that very moment we knew Harlan had transitioned from his earthly home to his heavenly one.

I believe God honors our truly seeking His face during these urgent and intense moments of life. However, I also believe God desires for His children to seek His face and His will consistently. He desires our heart and our focus all the time. In 2 Chronicles 12:14, it is said about King Rehoboam that "he did evil because he had not set his heart on seeking the LORD."

Setting our heart is a matter of focus. Coaches know full well many games are lost in the dimension of focus. Too many couples grapple with lost marriages due to lost focus. Successful businesses are punished by the marketplace due to unnecessary distraction or complacency that compromises focus. Vibrant and God-honoring missions and churches are spun into turmoil when focus is lost.

Likewise, teams succeed, marriages endure, businesses thrive, and missions are fulfilled because of crystal-clear focus. "Seek My face" is about focus . . . focus on God!

Jesus reinforces this principle in His famed Sermon on the Mount when He says "seek first his kingdom and his righteousness . . ." Simply put, God wants and desires top priority. And different from my agenda-laced prayers, He wants me and you to seek His will, not our own.

Too often, I find myself praying for my will. Again, I believe He wants to hear our goals and our desires. But in His words of "seek My face" and "set our hearts" and "seek first his kingdom," He is reminding us of who He is, and whose we are, as well as the proverbial flowchart of importance. It is His kingdom. It is His righteousness. It is His will . . . not ours. We are His people. We are called by His name.

David writes beautifully in Psalm 27 of his desire to

seek God's face, His kingdom, and His righteousness. In verse 4, he says, "One thing I ask of the LORD, this only do I seek: that I may dwell in the house of the LORD all the days of my life." As David seeks, his priorities are aligned. He has one focus and one request, to dwell in the house of the Lord.

In verse 8, David fervently prays, "My heart says of you, 'Seek his face!' Your face, LORD, I will seek. Do not hide your face from me, do not turn your servant away in anger; you have been my helper. Do not reject me or forsake me, God my Savior."

David knows his frailty and understands his status. He needs God; his heart is to seek His face, and he passionately wants God to be there for him.

God desires the same sincerity from us in this revival verse. Yes, there are important and urgent issues facing our country. Our fiscal deficit is great, and our moral deficit is greater. We have instructed our children to "build bigger barns" versus abiding by God's precepts (Luke 12:18). We desperately desire His divine intervention to spare our children and to bless our country.

And as we pray for our country's revival and awakening, He is saying to set our heart to "seek His face" in all aspects of our lives—from our personal relationship with Him, to our marriages that honor Him, to our parenting that teaches about Him, to tithing our time and possessions that prioritize Him, and to us as the Church that draw others to Him through truth and love.

If we earnestly desire revival, we must set our hearts to seek His face!

CHAPTER 8

"AND TURN FROM THEIR WICKED WAYS"

There is a growing conviction everywhere,
and especially among thoughtful people,
that unless revival comes,
other forces will take the field,
that will sink us still deeper
into the mire of humanism and materialism.

DUNCAN CAMPBELL

"And Turn from Their Wicked Ways"

We like to point the finger toward someone else. They are to blame. They are the reason God is removing His hedge of protection from our country. They have caused our fiscal cliffs and moral compromises. They are the ones who spit in God's face instead of seeking His face. They, they, they are to blame! Hold on. This verse is telling God's people, who bear His name, to turn from their wicked ways. This means you. This means me.

The apostle Paul is a hero to people of faith. His knowledge, his sacrifices, his bold and courageous spirit as he spread the Gospel, and his enduring zeal to persevere are inspiring. Yet Paul says he is the worst of the worst when it comes to sinning. When describing the reason Christ Jesus came to this world, Paul writes in his first letter to Timothy that Christ came to save sinners, "of whom I am the worst" (1 Timothy 1:15).

I believe that Paul, just as Isaiah did in Isaiah 6, realizes how unclean he is and how far he is from a holy, holy God due to encountering and embracing the one true God. When believers pause and gaze upon the face of God, we quickly realize how ruined we are as a people, and how ruined our culture is as well. We cannot measure up to a holy and righteous God. This is why we need a Savior.

The apostle John instructs us, "If we claim to be without sin, we deceive ourselves and the truth is not in us. If we confess our sins, He is faithful and just and will forgive our sins and purify us from all unrighteousness. If we claim we have not sinned, we make him out to be a liar and his word is not in us" (1 John 1:8–10).

Simply put, we are sinners. Yes, it is easier and personally more comforting to point out the grievous sins of others that are causing the downward spiral in our culture. However, God wants us to recognize, repent, and address the sin in our own lives for revival. My hunch is He desires for us to be a genuine article when bearing His name, versus an "in name only" believer who is quickly disqualified.

Jesus, again in the Sermon on the Mount, warns us against going after the speck of sawdust in our brother's eye, while glaring around with a plank of wood in our own eye (Matthew 7:4). God and Jesus are one in message as they are one in the Trinity. Their words reflect authenticity when it comes to our human frailty and our need for humility, repentance, and redemption.

Paul sums up our sinful nature and life in Romans 7 when he writes,

For I know that good itself does not dwell in me, that is, in my sinful nature. For I have the desire to

do what is good, but I cannot carry it out. For I do not do the good I want to do, but the evil I do not want to do—this I keep on doing. Now if I do what I do not want to do, it is no longer I who do it, but it is sin living in me that does it. So I find this law at work: Although I want to do good, evil is right there with me.

I don't know about you, but I do know about me, and I can so identify with Paul's desire disorder. I want to do good, but I so often do the opposite. I desperately don't want to sin, but so often cave to my sinful nature. You name the sin, I suffer from most of them: pride, lust, greed, deception, and anger are only the beginning of a long list of the turns I need to maneuver to honor God in this revival call.

This is why Paul goes on to say that he needs to die to himself daily. He needs to stay focused in prayer, washed in God's Word, active in the Christian community, to be unafraid, and to constantly remember God's faithfulness. He reiterates his need for focus in his first letter to the church in Corinth, chapter 9, beginning in verse 24:

Do you not know that in a race all the runners run, but only one gets the prize? Run in such a way as to get the prize. Everyone who competes in the games goes into strict training. They do it to get a crown that will not last, but we do it to get a crown that will last forever. Therefore I do not run like someone running aimlessly; I do not fight like a boxer beating the air. No, I strike a blow to my body and make it my slave so that after I have preached to others, I myself will not be disqualified for the prize.

Here Paul states what every successful athlete embraces. Strict training produces results. The intentional weight lifting, nutritional regiment, agility exercises, speed intervals, endurance runs, and skill repetition are implemented in a manner to produce peak performance. In like manner, seeking God's face in prayer, daily partaking in His Word, meaningful fasting, worshiping in community, and righteous living are key training elements to authentically seeking God's face and turning from our wicked ways.

Focus, focus, focus is the key to fulfillment. As a coach, I instructed my players to focus for four quarters, eight minutes per quarter, thirty-two minutes per game, so that our chance for victory would be greatly enhanced. Focus is key to success, fulfillment, and experiencing new heights in all aspects of life, including turning from our wicked ways.

I observed this firsthand when our youngest son, Logan, was six years old. We took our boys to visit my sister who lived in Michigan. She took us to the local mall, which had a massive rock climbing wall. Now, being Dutch, I don't part with money easily, but we were on vacation and I was feeling generous, so I told the boys that we would pay for them to climb the wall. Logan, our little white tornado, was the only one to accept the challenge. He was six years old and fearless. He had been observing teenagers and adults attempting to reach the top, lose their grip, and fall away from the wall at the same protruding point every time. But he was ready to go!

As they strapped on his harness, Logan looked up at me and asked if I was planning to climb with him. "Uh-huh. I'm not climbing any wall," I said, "but I'll be right here to encourage you and talk you through it." A few moments later he was on his way up, and I was cheering him on. "Hey, good job, Logan! Push off with your left foot. Now reach up with your right hand. Grab on. Hold on tight."

Our family's cameras were working overtime, and, to my surprise, Logan was doing pretty well. As he reached the section of the wall that had defeated most adults, he grabbed on tight, trying to move to safety, but suddenly let go. The belt around his small body suspended him far above our heads, inches from the wall. I thought, *Oh well, it was a good attempt, but that's it.* What impressed me is that Logan never looked away. He never looked down. He just stared at the wall, reached for it, and persisted climbing. I stood there, looking up at him, thinking, *You stud!*

He continued climbing until he reached the top, giving it a slap of victory, and I started yelling, "That's my son!" After his descent as we waited for them to remove his harness, we began to discuss his accomplishment. Why could Logan, a scrawny six-year-old, conquer the wall when teenagers and adults were unable to do so? Darla assessed it beautifully, saying, "Because he has incredible focus when he chooses to apply it."

And as coaches coach, teachers teach, leaders encourage, and Paul reminds us, things tend to turn out well when we focus. It is our distractions that compromise our integrity, that sell out our values, that shuffle our priorities, and that crash relationships.

As I read Old Testament Scripture, I always marvel, and at times laugh, at the forgetful nature of the Israelites. They witnessed God speak in a cloud, they were on the shore when the Red Sea parted, they heard the trumpets, the thunder, and witnessed the lightning when they saw Moses descend the mountain with the Ten Commandments. They were fed with food that fell from the sky. They were delivered from the bondage of the Egyptians. And, yet, they would get distracted and take their focus off of their Provider, off of their Defender, off of their God.

How could they, I boastfully ask? But, then again, it sounds a lot like me. My guess is it that it sounds a lot like you, too.

To me there is no better scripture from God to His people than Deuteronomy 8:6–20. It was God's desire for His people to partake in proper living in the land that flows with milk and honey. I urge you to read the scripture as italicized below with God's people, the New Covenant found in Christ, and America in mind:

> *Observe the commands of the Lord your God, walking in obedience to him and revering him. For the Lord your God is bringing you into a good land—a land with brooks, streams, and deep springs gushing out into the valleys and hills; a land with wheat and barley, vines and fig trees, pomegranates, olive oil and honey; a land where bread will not be scarce and you will lack nothing; a land where the rocks are iron and you can dig copper out of the hills.*

When you have eaten and are satisfied, praise the Lord *your God for the good land he has given you. Be careful that you do not forget the* Lord *your God, failing to observe his commands, his laws and his decrees that I am giving you this day. Otherwise, when you eat and are satisfied, when you build fine houses and settle down, and when your herds and flocks grow large and your silver and gold increase and all you have is multiplied, then your heart will become proud and you will forget the* Lord *your God, who brought you out of Egypt, out of the land of slavery. He led you through the vast and dreadful wilderness, that thirsty and waterless land, with its venomous snakes and scorpions. He brought you water out of hard rock. He gave you manna to eat in the wilderness, something your ancestors had never known, to humble and test you so that in the end it might go well with you. You may say to yourself, "My power and the strength of my hands have produced this wealth for me." But remember the* Lord *your God, for it is he who gives you the ability to produce wealth, and so confirms his covenant, which he swore to your ancestors, as it is today.*

If you ever forget the Lord *your God and follow other gods and worship and bow down to them, I testify against you today that you will surely be destroyed. Like the nations the* Lord *destroyed before you, so you will be destroyed for not obeying the* Lord *your God.*

As I read these verses, I can't help but think we have lost focus on our Provider, our Deliverer, and our God through our prosperity. I believe God is calling us to remember . . . Him. I believe God is calling us to repent. God is calling us to action. He wants us to "turn" from our wicked ways.

When driving a car, turning to the left or to the right is a deliberate and intentional act. Thus, it is when we turn from our wicked ways. God wants us to be deliberate and intentional as we follow through on our return to, and our focus on, Him. By turning from our wicked ways . . . from self to Him . . . in full pursuit of His kingdom and His righteousness, we are making a deliberate and intentional choice.

Let it begin . . . with me . . . with you . . . with US!

CHAPTER 9

"THEN I WILL HEAR FROM HEAVEN"

Open the blind eyes
Unlock the deaf ears
Come to your people
As we draw near
Hear us from heaven
Touch our generation
We are your people
Crying out in desperation

"Hear Us from Heaven" by Jared Anderson

⁜

CHAPTER 9

"Then I Will Hear from Heaven"

We started this book with the little two-letter word *if*. And as important in meaning as the word *if* is, the four-letter word *then* is huge!

The word *if* sets the prerequisites: *If* God's people humble themselves and *if* God's people pray and *if* God's people turn from their wicked ways. The *if* is the catalyst for the desired action. And *if* we take action, the *then* activates the promises. In this case, the desired revival.

Hold on, because the rest of this verse describes God's promises. First and foremost, He promises to hear our prayers. The authenticity and sincerity that God seeks culminates into a promise of, "I'll listen to your prayers." The God of the universe, our Creator, the Alpha and Omega, Immanuel, and the Great I Am says, "Once I see the authenticity of your heart . . . I will hear your prayer." Take a moment to breathe that in. . . . Wow!

When I was a CEO serving young men and women with traumatic brain injury, I would witness less than desirable behaviors because staff and clients were not listening to what each other were saying. When I was a high school principal, I sat through endless meetings and counseling sessions attempting to resolve disputes with the students, the teachers, and the parents by structuring an environment where each one could be heard.

Marriages end in divorce, customers get lost, and wars get launched when people tire of not being heard. Have you ever been to an exhaustion point in your communication when you express through frustration, "Are you hearing what I am saying?"

Good news . . . God is saying yes. If you're sincere, if you're authentic, if you're humble, and if you are taking action to rid sin from your life, then yes, He promises to hear your prayers. He is gazing into your heart.

This verse says, "Then I will hear from heaven." After being assured God will hear our prayers, God reminds us of His location . . . heaven. In Isaiah 55:8–9, the prophet confirms why God provides us an Old Testament GPS of His locale. God assures in this familiar passage that His thoughts are not our thoughts and that His ways are not our ways. He then concludes by reassuring us that as the heavens are higher than the earth, so His ways are higher than our ways, and His thoughts higher than our thoughts. He is God, and He is in charge and in control.

Translation: Our desired response on earth may not mesh with His desire in heaven. Since He is God and we are not, we must trust Him.

The Old Testament character Hannah understood this concept, as her story recorded in 1 Samuel 1 indicates. For some reason her womb was closed, which made it impossible for her to have children. Hannah, as is true of many barren women, was deeply distraught over the inability to have sons and daughters. But unlike most women today, Hannah had another grievance. Her husband, Elkanah, and his other wife, Peninnah, provoked and nagged her about not being able to conceive a child, until Hannah wept and refused to eat.

Hannah desperately wanted God to hear her prayer for a son. She poured herself out before the Lord. Scripture says in verse 10 that in bitterness of soul Hannah wept much and prayed to the Lord. In her prayer, she made a promise to the Lord that should He fulfill her request, she would dedicate her son all of his days to the service of the Lord.

Hannah's prayer was intense. As she wept, her lips moved but no audible voice could be heard. At this time, Eli the priest confronted Hannah about a possible drinking problem. Eli assumed that Hannah must be drunk, because she was weeping and mouthing words without talking.

When Eli discovered that Hannah's prayer came from deep within her heart, he told her to go in peace with the blessing that God would grant her request. Well, the rest is history. Hannah became pregnant and bore a son whom she and Elkanah named Samuel.

The sincerity and authenticity of Hannah's prayer could not be more real. God heard her prayer and blessed her with a son, and Hannah blessed God by dedicating Samuel's life to the service of the Lord.

I believe it is wise to insert a cautionary flag at this point. If we study this story on the surface, it is rational to conclude that if we weep and pour out our soul, God will give us what we want. However, the true test is the measure of the heart. Our heart must be for God's perfect will. Hannah's heart was in sync with God's heart . . . with or without child.

Jesus' prayer, the night before His crucifixion in the garden of Gethsemane, illustrates this point. His prayer was so sincere that we are told "his sweat was like drops of blood falling to the ground" (Luke 22:44). His words were chilling as He prayed that the Father would take this cup from Him. However, notice He follows His plea with a submission to God's will. God didn't remove the cup, and we as believers have the promise of eternal life as a result.

As God searches our hearts, Jesus offers several glimpses of God's heart when we pray. In Luke 11, He tells us to ask, to seek, and to knock. And when we do, our request will be given. We will find what we were searching for. The door will open. The action step is given to us, but our God is faithful, and He will hear and answer our prayer.

Jesus continues by paralleling an earthly father scenario. He asks, "Which of you fathers, if your son asks for a fish, will give him a snake instead? Or if he asks for an egg, will give him a scorpion?" (Luke 11:11–12). The obvious answer is no. As parents, we want to bless our child's request if it is in his or her best interest. The same is true of our Father in heaven. The difference is, we are failed parents and our Father in heaven is perfect, true, constant, and holy. Above all, He is faithful and can be trusted.

The best example I can conjure that illustrates being at peace with God's will for an earthly request is the Old Testament favorite found in the first three chapters of Daniel, and particularly the story of Shadrach, Meshach, Abednego and the fiery furnace. These three young men were living in exile in Babylon. Not only were they exiled in a foreign land, they were given new names and new identities in order to strip them of any Jerusalem tie.

These three young men along with Daniel were a cut above the rest when Judah was captured by Nebuchadnezzar's Babylon. Because of this, they were put into strict training so they could serve in Nebuchadnezzar's court and at the king's command. Daniel was a flat-out stud and gained much favor with the king after revealing the king's dream and its meaning. Because of Daniel, young guns Shadrach, Meshach, and Abednego became administrators over the province of Babylon while Daniel remained at the royal court.

By all accounts, even though they were exiled and stripped of their families and identities, this rapid advancement was some pretty heady stuff for such young men in a new land.

To say King Nebuchadnezzar got a little too full of himself is an understatement. He built a 90' golden statue to signify himself and his kingdom. Upon an old-time "executive order," he required that everyone bow down to this statue when they heard the music play. There were no exceptions to the "bow down" rule. Administrators, judges, advisers, treasurers, and all other provincial officials had to join in the bended knee musical ceremony.

However, after the music played in perfect harmony, the three young guns from Judah stayed standing. Immediately, they were brought to King Nebuchadnezzar. He gave them one more opportunity to take a knee upon hearing the music. If they did not comply, they were told they would be thrown into the fiery furnace.

All of this is cool, but here is what is really cool. Nebuchadnezzar had barely gotten the threat of the scorching fire and death out his mouth, when they assured him that they would never bow down to this false god. Meshach, Shadrach, and Abednego were confident that their God would rescue them. And they assured the king that even if their God chose not to spare them, they were never going to bow down to the false god.

You talk about guts. The province of Babylon is shaking in their boots and bending their knees to the music, and the three young exiles say no.

We can learn a lot from these young men. Everywhere we turn today in our modern world, we are encouraged to do what's right in our own eyes. In our society we are told to get with it and to catch up with the times, with the culture, and with the polls. In other words, forsake your God and the pursuit of His righteousness, and bow down to the god and the golden statues of today . . . bow to self and our own indulgences.

I believe that Daniel, who faced the threat of a lion, and his three amigos, who faced the heat of the fiery furnace, would tell us, "Even if everyone else is embracing false gods, stand tall for the one true God."

Quite frankly, I think our culture could use a few Daniels and a few hundred or thousand or million Shadrachs, Meshachs, and Abednegos.

God, in heaven, heard the prayers of Hannah, of Daniel and his friends, and of Jesus, His Son. In this verse, He promises to hear our prayers, too.

We just need to set our heart in seeking Him. And as we seek Him, it may be good medicine to keep humming that old Sunday school song, "Though none go with me, still I will follow."

Are you ready to say, "Here I am . . . I'm standing . . . I'm praying . . . I'm believing"?

CHAPTER 10

"AND FORGIVE THEIR SINS"

For He rescued us
from the domain of darkness,
and transferred us to
the kingdom of His beloved Son,
in whom we have redemption,
the forgiveness of sins.

COLOSSIANS 1:13–14 NASB

CHAPTER 10

"And Forgive Their Sins"

As she knelt before him with her hands in front of her face, she begged him not to do it. However, in a fit of rage, he did it. He pulled the trigger of his dad's shotgun and shot his girlfriend of three years in the face. After a few days in the Intensive Care and a fatal diagnosis, her parents pulled the plug. She died, and it was his fault. He killed her.

It is a story of any parent's worst nightmare. Your child senselessly lost due to a mindless act of violence. The parents of this girl were immediately incensed. They had every right to be. And the parents of her boyfriend, their son, were shocked and in disbelief at the news. They were in love as a boyfriend and girlfriend; it didn't, and it still doesn't, make sense. Nevertheless, promising lives are taken. The girl is dead, and the boy is headed for a life behind bars.

The twist of the story as told in *The New York Times* is forgiveness. As the girl's dad held his daughter's hand in the ICU, he could sense her saying, "Forgive him." Immediately, he thought, *Never*. However, he describes the repeated "forgive him" sensations from his daughter.

And that's what they did . . . they forgave the killer. Through hugs, through tears, through words, and through a deep faith, they forgave him. They, along with his parents, met with a mediator and prosecuting attorney, pleading for restorative justice in a tough Florida penal system. And the net result, instead of the death penalty he received a prison sentence of twenty years and ten years of probation.

It had to be tough to hear the story retold. But they listened and they cried and they got angry and they continued to forgive him. For them, it is a release and a transition from the daughter being a victim of murder to her life living on with purpose, with love, with faith, and with forgiveness.

This story goes against human nature. Our nature is for revenge. If we've been wronged, our nature is to have the focus placed on the payment we are owed. These parents turned the story on its head by forgiving, by letting go, and by moving on in faith. This faith story gives legs to "forgive us our trespasses (our debts) as we forgive those who trespass against us (our debtors)."

The boyfriend, the son, the murderer, knew he didn't deserve the parents' or the state's grace. But he received it through words, through action, through hugs, through prayers, and through a greatly reduced sentence.

If you are "wowed" by this story as I was, you should be. Forgiveness is the "wow" factor. Whether it's a murder or adultery or theft or deception, forgiveness is the transition to full restoration. It takes a "wow" to make it happen! And when it does happen, it makes news—in this case, ten pages on *The New York Times* website. Forgiveness is rare, it's special, and when it's realized, it's celebrated.

Jesus provided a forgiveness "wow" of His own when He showed up at the temple courts to teach on the Sabbath (read John 8). While He was there, the teachers of the law and the Pharisees brought a woman caught in the act of adultery to the temple courts for public humiliation and to test Jesus.

They interrogated Jesus regarding the law of Moses. They recited the laws to remind Jesus of their meaning. The law was clear. This woman was to be stoned.

The rulers were trumpeting righteous judgment. The woman fearfully shook in shame and fear. And Jesus seized the moment to teach.

As the Pharisees continued their babbling, Jesus looked down and began writing in the sand. Maybe His lack of eye contact and scribbling was to communicate boredom with their thirst for theater. Or maybe it was to insinuate knowledge regarding their personal lack of integrity with their accusation.

Regardless of His reason, the verbal message He delivered was clearly heard. When Jesus straightened His posture and looked at them, He said, "If any one of you is without sin, let him be the first to throw a stone at her." One by one they dropped their stones and exited the temple courts. Everyone left until it was just Jesus and the woman.

The woman was stunned, and the people who gathered for their Sunday service were amazed. It is a sermon that gets repeated frequently to this day. The service had an audience, it had drama, it had confrontation of sin, it was filled with Truth, and it had a lasting message. Now, that's a sermon! All the service was missing was the organ music and the offering!

Once the temple courts cleared, Jesus was left alone with the adulterous woman. He had the opportunity to meet her where she was at. Undoubtedly, Jesus had a fair advantage. He just saved her with His teaching. She owed Him her life.

The woman knew what she did was wrong. She knew she deserved to be punished. However, miraculously her accusers dropped their cause, and their stones, because of Jesus' teaching.

Being the master Teacher, Jesus continues His lesson by asking the woman the obvious, "Where are they? Has no one condemned you?" Her reply is a nervous, "No one, sir." Now for the trump card—the only one without sin and with the power to condemn says, "Then neither do I condemn you." Wow!

But wait, class isn't over yet. Jesus continues by telling her, "Go now and leave your life of sin." He does this out of His genuine love for her. This sin is hurting her, soiling her reputation, and damaging her mental health.

My guess is that she absorbed this message with great relief and with great intrigue . . . such as, "Who are you?" and "Where did you come from?" and "What are you doing here?" All she really knew was that she was never going to be the same. For the first time in a long time she felt what love really is . . . and it came through forgiveness. Wow!

Believers share the idea that we, as a country, are in need of a "wow" . . . God's forgiveness. We realize that instead of pursuing God's kingdom and His righteousness, we have been in full pursuit of our individual and earthly kingdoms and our endless indulgences. This pursuit has resulted in an intense and mountainous moral crisis on every fiscal and social horizon. Intuitively, we know only God holds the answer through His power to forgive.

It is only natural for us to think that forgiveness is out of reach, because we realize how undeserving we are as a people. However, time and again via Scripture we recognize that forgiveness is in God's character. The revival verse of 2 Chronicles 7:14 says it, and over and over again in Scripture God highlights it, and His actions prove it.

Forgiveness for us as His people and for our country is within reach. I believe it is His heart, and it is His desire!

The ultimate proof and picture of forgiveness is in His Son, our Savior and our Lord, Jesus Christ. John 3:16 is as true today as it was when it was penned by John the Apostle in approximately A.D. 90, "For God so loved the world that he gave his one and only Son, that whoever believes in him shall not perish but have eternal life."

We know our human condition and our sinful nature. We know that we in and of ourselves don't deserve this forgiveness. However, God's heart is of love, of redemption, of restoration, and of forgiveness. God does whatever it takes to draw us back to Him, even sending His Son from heaven to earth, from life to a cruel death, and from a tomb to glory. Talk about a "WOW" factor!

If this is His heart for you and for me, doesn't it make sense that this is His heart for our country, for our land, and for our people?

I believe there is great similarity as to where we are as a country today and the story of the "prodigal son," as told by Jesus in Luke 15 to the tax collectors and the sinners within earshot of the Pharisees and the teachers of the law.

The story is about a dad who worked hard, was diligent, and intentional about developing a business. He was blessed with two boys whom he included in the business. As the boys learned the business, they undoubtedly became knowledgeable of their dad's success and his vast accumulation.

One of the sons desired to model himself after his dad. He worked hard and invested his talents with the vision of long-term harvest. However, the younger son wasn't motivated by the growth of the business. Instead, he was motivated by the accumulation of great wealth and the indulgences it could afford. Adding to his misguided motivation was his brashness as he approached his father with an "entitlement mentality" and demanded his full share of the estate. His goals were to cash the check, cut the family ties, relocate to an exotic place, and indulge himself on his dad's success, all within his own rules and terms. Sound familiar?

The father relents and allows the son to exercise his free

will. The son grabs the cash and parties like it's 1999. He recklessly spends his share of the wealth on self-absorbed living. Much to his surprise, the money didn't last, and an unexpected drought and famine set in the land. Not only was he out of money, but he was out of food, and he was far away from his family.

In an effort to survive, he hired himself out to feed pigs. As he fed the pigs, he realized that the pigs were eating better than he was. He was hungry, broke, and at the end of himself. He had nowhere else to turn but back to his dad.

As he journeyed back to the homeland, he planned to come clean with his father in full humility. He was going to let him know everything—how he squandered the wealth, how he was broke, and how he didn't deserve to be called his son. He now only aspired to be taken back and to be given a job as a hired hand. The entitlement mentality was gone, replaced by reality and the goals for basic food, shelter, clothing, and family.

What makes this story special is that Jesus paints a portrait of the heart of God in the father's response. The son hasn't even made it home yet, and obviously he hasn't said a word. However, as soon as the father sees his son on the road making his way toward home, he runs to him. He drops everything and runs. He drops everything and embraces his son. He drops everything and throws a party to end all parties!

He drops everything and forgives. Wow!

As parents, we can relate to this heart. We love our

children dearly. If anything separates us, we long for their return, for their embrace, and for their fellowship. This is what makes us family.

God is pleading for us, His people, His family to return home. And just like the famous story, I believe He desires to run to us, to embrace us, and to throw us a party. He is a God of love. He is a God of forgiveness. And He is a God of restoration.

Wow!

CHAPTER 11

"AND HEAL THEIR LAND"

Healing rain is coming down
It's coming closer to the lost and found
Tears of joy, and tears of shame
Are washed forever in Jesus' name
Healing rain, it comes with fire
So let it fall and take us higher
Healing rain, I'm not afraid
To be washed in Heaven's rain

"Healing Rain" by Michael W. Smith

CHAPTER 11

"And Heal Their Land"

"America the Beautiful" is the song they sang. They sang it before the Super Bowl. I've heard the song many times, and I have witnessed most Super Bowl pregame ceremonies for the past thirty years. However, the pregame program highlighting this Super Bowl was extra-ordinary. It featured the children of Sandy Hook Elementary. And as they sang the words, "God shed His grace on thee," you could sense America's collective throat lumping and eyes tearing.

Almost two months before the Super Bowl, in the quiet and safe neighborhoods of Newtown, Connecticut, Sandy Hook Elementary was thrust into the world's spotlight via a senseless and evil act of violence that left twenty-six dead . . . twenty of them elementary-aged children. Families were devastated, a community sent reeling, and our country is still searching for answers.

And now, on this hyped-up American tradition, the family of Sandy Hook sang the answer . . . "God Shed His Grace on Thee." This is the trademark of God's promise to heal . . . His grace.

Fifty years ago a segment of our America was in search of God's grace. Their spokesman was eloquent and spiritually grounded. In his famous "I Have a Dream" speech, Martin Luther King implored his followers, black and white, to dream of a free America, but to do it in a manner that honored the God whom they served.

Sit back and take a listen to a couple of excerpts:

> *"But there is something that I must say to my people who stand on the warm threshold which leads into the palace of justice. In the process of gaining our rightful place we must not be guilty of wrongful deeds. Let us not seek to satisfy our thirst for freedom by drinking from the cup of bitterness and hatred."*

After setting this God-honoring standard for process, he unveiled his dream:

> *"I say to you today, my friends, that in spite of the difficulties and frustrations of the moment, I still have a dream. It is a dream deeply rooted in the American dream.*
>
> *"I have a dream that one day this nation will rise up and live out the true meaning of its creed: 'We hold these truths to be self-evident: that all men are created equal.'*
>
> *"I have a dream that one day on the red hills of Georgia the sons of former slaves and the sons of former slave owners will be able to sit down together at a table of brotherhood.*

"I have a dream that one day even the state of Mississippi, a desert state, sweltering with the heat of injustice and oppression, will be transformed into an oasis of freedom and justice.

"I have a dream that my four children will one day live in a nation where they will not be judged by the color of their skin but by the content of their character.

"I have a dream today.

"I have a dream that one day the state of Alabama, whose governor's lips are presently dripping with the words of interposition and nullification, will be transformed into a situation where little black boys and black girls will be able to join hands with little white boys and white girls and walk together as sisters and brothers.

"I have a dream today.

"I have a dream that one day every valley shall be exalted, every hill and mountain shall be made low, the rough places will be made plain, and the crooked places will be made straight, and the glory of the Lord shall be revealed, and all flesh shall see it together."

As King communicates his dream, you can see the America he envisions. Many leaders say that followers must see it in order to believe it. King most certainly delivered on portraying this compelling picture to his followers.

Using King as inspiration, I believe God's people must

likewise have a dream for a healed land. Jesus provides us the starting point in His Sermon on the Mount address found in Matthew 6:33,

> *"But seek first his kingdom and his righteousness, and all these things will be given to you as well."*

So often our focus is on the desired end. Jesus says to refocus and put your priorities in order, God's kingdom and His righteousness. Then the churches will be filled, then families will flourish, then marriages will be honored, then life will be sacred, then crops will be bountiful, then government will be limited, then financial debt will be erased, then hard work will be valued, then talents will be maximized, then streets will be safe, then children will be properly nurtured and educated by their parents, then widows and orphans will be embraced, then the homeless will be given shelter, then the naked will be clothed, and then all the hungry will be fed. And the *then* ripples continue and continue when we seek first.

Tom Brokaw coined the World War II generation as "the Greatest Generation." He may have coined this generation, but the rest of us who know them readily agreed. Why? Because we witnessed firsthand how they put others ahead of themselves. They embodied self-sacrifice when it came to their faith, to their marriages, to their families, to their communities, and to their country. What made them great was the ability to put "the cause above themselves." This, in my opinion, sums up leadership at any level, "cause above self."

Likewise, Christ is calling God's people to take the focus off themselves and to place it on God, His kingdom, and His righteousness. Things will look different on Pennsylvania Avenue, on K Street, on Wall Street, on Main Street, and on your street when we set our sights with an eternal versus earthly focus.

Thus, I dream of an America where we lift God's name above all names. Where we honor Him in thought, in word, and in deed. And we openly acknowledge Him with our praise and thanksgiving for His blessings on our land and on us as a people.

I dream of an America where we remember the Sabbath day by going to church, by resting from our daily routines to refocus our energy, our lives, and our families on Him.

I dream of an America where children listen to and respect their moms and their dads. Where moms and dads teach their children God's principles, precepts, and love for them in the morning, throughout the day, and when they go to bed at night, instilling a legacy of faith from generation to generation.

I dream of an America that cherishes the gift of life. An America that acknowledges God as the Author and Creator of all human life. An America that esteems each day as ordained and planned before one day is ever lived.

I dream of an America where husbands love their wives enough to die for them, and where wives respect their husbands.

I dream of an America where doors remain unlocked and where visitors are welcomed to our homes, to our cars, and to our possessions.

I dream of an America where our words are our bond. Where our yes is yes and our no is no, and there is no need for written contracts or lawyers.

I dream of an America where we live content with the blessings we receive from our talent, our ability, our home, our clothes, our family, our surroundings, and our Treasurer.

I dream of an America that gives generously and lives with a focus on eternity.

I dream of an America that embodies and lives by the fruit of the Spirit; love, joy, peace, longsuffering, kindness, goodness, faithfulness, meekness, and self-control.

I dream of an America that is patient, that is kind, that does not envy nor does it boast, that is not proud, that is not rude, that is not self-seeking, that is not easily angered, that keeps no record of wrongs, that does not delight in evil but rejoices in truth.

I dream of an America that always protects, always trusts, always hopes, and always perseveres.

I dream of an America overflowing with faith, with hope, and with love.

I dream of an America where the saving grace found in Jesus Christ is fully embraced.

I dream of an America where God's people who are called by His name humble themselves and pray and turn from their wicked ways and of an America where God hears the prayers and forgives our sins and heals our land.

I dream of this America.

Call to Action

Where were you?

Most adults I know can readily recall where they were when two hijacked jetliners deliberately tore through the Twin Towers in New York City on September 11, 2001. Not only can they tell you with great precision about their whereabouts, but they can relive in great detail their thoughts, their emotions, their shock, and their prayers when our country became visibly under attack.

The common theme that emerged from all the stories is an unexpected feeling of unity. The things that divided us, as Americans, no longer seemed that important. There were no more Republican or Democrats, but rather a coming together as Americans. We were under attack, and we needed each other.

Our elected officeholders demonstrated this as they sang, "God Bless America," on the steps of the U.S. Capitol. President Bush galvanized us as a country with his immediate words, actions, and decisive leadership.

The New York City fire department, police department, port authority, and countless others inspired us with their heroism on behalf of their fellow Americans. While many were running from the devastation, they were running toward the devastation. There was a spirit in the air . . . it was an "American Spirit" demonstrated by these brave men and women who brought us together as "one."

Our collective response to this attack was to fill the chapels and sanctuaries for prayer, comfort, blessing, and protection. It was the first time I can recall when I had to stand outside of a chapel because of the overflow attendance. I couldn't hear all the prayers, but I could sense a unity in prayer. After the service, I walked across the chapel grounds with many that day, in silence . . . in humility . . . in a continued attitude of prayer as the chapel bells played a solemn hymn.

The churches and chapels were filled because people had their sense of security and comfort shattered; in other words, they briefly woke up from complacency. There was a sense of desperation and dependence on not just God, but specifically what He offers us in Christ: forgiveness of our sins and the hope of eternal life.

True revival begins with the personal acceptance of Jesus Christ, God's one and only Son . . . who lived, who died, and who rose again . . . so that whoever believes in Him shall not perish but have eternal life (John 3:16).

Apart from receiving Jesus Christ, revival is impossible.

Thus, a most fitting tribute to all these emotions and feelings of dependency on 9/11 was a makeshift cross, which was erected at Ground Zero. Why? It provides hope. And it serves as a symbol that when God is the only answer, nothing else will do.

As one elder statesman told me, "When we have nowhere to run and nowhere to hide, we turn to God."

Today, similarly, we know that our country, our values, our morals, and God's righteousness are under attack. It's just not as blatant or as obvious as a single event such as 9/11. When 9/11 happened, all the news . . . all the time . . . covered the devastation. We felt it, we sensed it, we were on edge.

Today, the mainstream media shields the attack, or even celebrates the moral drift away from God and to government and to ourselves. It seems as if we insulate ourselves from this drift, in near total denial. And, if it doesn't affect me . . . then, who am I to care?

However, when we stop to reflect, we know there must be something more, and we know nothing short of revival will do. This is why The FAMiLY LEADER committed to write *If 7:14*, and why we are launching the "If 7:14 Initiative." It is a high calling to stand in the gap for the next generations, and this revival verse provides us a template.

I hope that after reading these chapters, you will join The FAMiLY LEADER team and me in answering the call by saying, "I will." "I will" pray for personal revival, for revival in our marriages, for revival in our families, for revival in our churches, for revival in our communities, for revival in our country, and for revival in our world. As mentioned earlier in this book, revival is an inside-out calling. God wants you, me, us . . . all of us!

He wants our heart, our soul, our mind, and our strength. He wants us to demonstrate our sincerity of devotion through our humility, prayers, seeking His face, and authentic repentance by turning from our wicked (indifferent) ways. He wants us to be absolutely devoted to Him!

I don't know about you, but I do know about me. I'm busy. I have meetings, dinners, church, small group, Bible studies, family activities, youth sports, vacations, travel, home chores, and many volunteer opportunities.

The irony is that when I look at my "to do" list, it is filled with good things. And the reality of this "to do" list is that the items I schedule are most likely the ones I get accomplished, while the many things I'd like to do, but don't schedule, represent a mixed bag of results.

Thus, I suggest you schedule your revival prayer times. Through our "If 7:14 Initiative," we are urging God's people to rise up and to pray in unity at 7:14 a.m. and 7:14 p.m. Our growing If 7:14 team is setting our smartphones and other alarm devices to alert us at these times. And when the reminder goes off . . . we pray . . . we seek God's face . . . for repentance and revival.

I sincerely urge you to take this first step. Say "I will!" and join us in united prayer for revival at 7:14 a.m. and 7:14 p.m. wherever you may be.

Then, I urge you to engage your network, your small group, your Christmas card list, your church, your family, and all those with whom you have influence. When you're out for coffee in the morning and your alarm goes off, take a minute with your guests for a revival prayer. When you're out for dinner with friends and your alarm nudges you, take the risk and invite them to join you in a time of revival prayer.

And, finally, be an inspiration to others praying for revival, by sharing your stories of revived lives, revived marriages, revived churches, etc. at www.If714.com. Let us commit to spur one another on . . . to love . . . to good deeds . . . to revival!

Where were you?

I believe many of us will be asked this simple, yet penetrating question, by our children and grandchildren some day in the not too distant future. When they review and critique this pivotal time in our country's history, my guess is they will want to know our whereabouts. In addition, I believe they will want to know what action we took when we witnessed things spinning out of control.

The World War II generation is often referenced as "the Greatest Generation," because they boldly stepped into the gap when their country needed them. This is our time to boldly step in the gap for the present and subsequent generations.

Let us be found faithful . . . on our knees . . . praying for revival . . . as we choose to be a great generation!

If 7:14 . . . It's time!

Call to Action Summary

1. **ANSWER THE CALL** and say "I will."

2. **JOIN THE IF 7:14 TEAM** and pray for revival at 7:14 a.m. and 7:14 p.m. every day. Pray for personal revival, for revival in our marriages, our families, our churches, our communities, our country, and our world.

3. **ENGAGE YOUR NETWORK** to join you in this call to pray for revival.

4. **BE AN INSPIRATION TO OTHERS** by sharing your stories of revived lives, revived marriages, revived churches, etc. at www.If714.com.

Remember . . .

The call to pray for revival must begin with a saving knowledge of our Lord and Savior Jesus Christ. True revival begins with the personal acceptance of Jesus Christ, God's one and only Son . . . who lived, who died for our sins, and who rose again . . . so that whoever believes in Him shall not perish but have eternal life (John 3:16).

Apart from receiving Jesus Christ, revival is impossible. If you would like to know more about becoming a Christian, please visit If714.com.

If714.com

THE FAMiLY LEADER
Strengthening families...

The FAMiLY LEADER exists to strengthen families. We champion the principle that God is the ultimate leader of the family. Our goal at The FAMiLY LEADER is to honor and glorify God—not a political party, not a candidate, and not a program. TFL is a Christ-centered organization that leads with humility and service to strengthen and protect the family.

Six Strategies of The FAMiLY LEADER:

- Engage churches, civic influencers, and Christian citizens with truthful, consistent information
- Encourage pastors to address culturally relevant issues from a biblical perspective
- Strengthen marriages through marriage mentoring and education
- Protect and defend family values in the civic arena
- Provide free legal counsel to families, churches, and schools in cases of religious discrimination
- Develop civic, church, social, and family leaders, including the cultivation of Christian statesmen

The FAMiLY LEADER . . . a consistent, courageous voice in the churches, in the legislature, in the media, in the courtroom, in the public square . . . always standing for God's truth.

Contact us:
The FAMiLY LEADER
P.O. Box 42245
Urbandale, IA 50323
515.263.3495

Twitter: @TheFamilyLeader
Facebook: www.facebook.com/THEFAMILYLEADER
TheFamilyLeader.com

Also by
Bob Vander Plaats

Lucas Vander Plaats was severely disabled from birth. But through his silent instruction and patient example, he taught his family dozens of life-changing lessons. And now they want to share them with you.

A devotional full of compelling insight, *Light from Lucas* has something important to say to all of us—from the value of human life to why God allows suffering. It's a true story of how God uses the weakest among us to accomplish powerful works.

God to www.LightFromLucas.com for more information on this book.